Editorial

Over the years *PN Review* has featured ancient and modern poetry emerging from unfamiliar traditions and offered fresh takes on familiar ones. We are lucky to have readers with wide curiosity and with language skills to translate, interpret and advocate. Some of our favourite poets come from unusual traditions. In *PNR 247* Maitreyabandhu recalls Jane Yeh's 'A Short History of Migration' where

> pain is communal and historical. Yeh is the daughter of Taiwanese migrants, so the subject has personal significance too. But she will not indulge. The deadpan humour is used to devastating effect: 'We ate the same meal seventeen days in a row (pancakes).' Then later, 'We hindered our children with violins, bad haircuts, and diplomas.'

In this issue of *PNR* we approach, tentatively, a tradition we have not properly focused on before, the Taiwanese. Taiwan first appeared in our pages in 1990. We reported, 'Taiwan has a News Bureau Code stipulating that publications which "offend or instigate other people, and violate or blaspheme sacrificial rites" shall be prohibited from importation, translation and publication. By such criteria, Salman Rushdie's *The Satanic Verses* has been found wanting and is now prohibited. Meanwhile Venezuela has become the first Western country in which *The Satanic Verses* has been actually banned.'

Taiwan appears again three years later in a poem by D.J. Enright. And in 2017 we reported on a Taiwanese poetic scandal:

> Controversy flared in Taiwan (reported in *The China Post*, 1 February) when President Tsai Ing-wen's contribution to the annual spring couplet ceremony was criticized for being 'incorrect'. Her defenders preferred to call her structuring 'unusual'. The head of the National Museum of Taiwanese Literature applauded the President's attempt, increasing awareness of Taiwan's literary culture, but it wouldn't quite do as a spring couplet: 'The president's spring couplets could probably count as two lines of new year greetings, but couplets? Not so much.' A number of rules constrain the spring couplet in terms of number of characters per line, the lexical category of each character in relation to their corresponding characters, and the tone patterns: one line must reverse the tone pattern of the other. The President rooted her couplet in one by Lai He, the 'father of modern Taiwanese literature'. Her office expressed its respect for diverse opinions and wished everyone a happy spring.

Clearly neither poetics nor politics is an easy discipline. Up until a few decades ago, if we are to believe Shengchi-Hsu in this issue of *PNR*, even a well-educated citizen of Taiwan might have been hard-pressed to name key poets in a specifically Taiwanese tradition of poetry, much less engage in sophisticated discussion of poetic traditions and forms. They would of course have known the major Chinese poets of the past, but awareness of a distinct or distinctive Taiwanese tradition was rare.

In the 1950s poets vied with one another, advocating a range of schools and issuing manifestos. Among the most eloquent polemicists was Chi Hsien (紀弦) who, in rejecting the Chinese tradition and wedding contemporary Taiwanese poetry to Western poetic radicalisms, coined the phrase 'horizontal transplantation' – (橫的移植, *hengde yizhi*) – which he contrasted with a 'vertical inheritance'. Rejecting the Chinese traditions was for him an overdue declaration of independence. But the Western modernisms to which it aligned itself were already being dismantled in the West. To his foes, 'horizontal transplantation' and the attempt to join a universal rather than pursue a national or traditionalist course felt like willing subjugation to another kind of colonial pressure. Taiwan had already chalked up a number of colonial legacies, including far-off Dutch and more recent Japanese.

The inspired and inspiring task of the Museum of Taiwan Literature, established two decades ago and housed in a handsome colonial building from the Japanese period, has been one of reclamation, to quote its own statement of purpose, 'from indigenous Malayo-Polynesian, the Dutch, Koxinga, Qing, and Japanese ruling periods through modern times'. Unlike Chi Hsien, part of whose task was a deliberate erasure of some elements in the past, the Museum's mission is to preserve, restore and even revive. Its motto is 'Locally rooted – globally connected', and the local rootedness distinguishes it from Chi Hsien's programmatic internationalism. The connections the Museum seems to pursue begin in a restored self-knowledge and a consciousness of the wealth entailed in the discontinuities that constitute its tradition. It insists on its cultural difference from the poetry of the Chinese mainland. *PNR* features in this issue examples of the poetry in question, translated collaboratively between a Taiwanese writer with excellent English and a Canadian poet of Greek antecedents, a major translator of Cavafy, here fishing, to use C.H. Sisson's phrase, in other men's waters.

This August the team from the Creative Industries Policy and Evidence Centre in Glasgow that conducted the bleak 2022 survey of authors' incomes, issued a list of implausible recommendations on how to make the UK 'an attractive haven for writers'. The recommendations would certainly revolutionise, and destroy, the contemporary poetry world.

- Publishers should declare a commitment to a minimum wage for commissioned authors and parity of treatment for all demographic groups
- Publishers should circulate educational resources to ensure writers understand copyright and contractual law
- Publishers should accept mandatory, time-limited reversion rights
- Publishers should accept transparency and reporting obligations

The team also urges changes in tax and social insurance treatment – 'for instance state support insurance schemes for writers that level the conditions between employed and self-employed workers'.

The head of policy at the Creative Industries Policy and Evidence Centre said: 'It's important to note that the challenges facing authors and publishers in the UK are far from unique; the deteriorating financial situation appears to be part of a global trend. This is worrying of course, but it also presents UK policymakers with an opportunity. Corrective action could help the UK be a flourishing centre for creative talent if more generous working conditions for authors were considered. Contrary to some fears, the advancement of AI and the ever-growing digital entertainment industry could lead to a higher demand for the authentic, creative voices of a diverse pool of writers.' The problem is, policymakers are not the writers who risk writing or the publishers who take them to market. Perhaps the experiment can be trialled in Scotland.

Letters to the editor

Dave Wynne-Jones writes: I was surprised to read 'The Con of the Wild' in *PN Review* 271. The argument of the article is full of holes but to treat it to a point by point rebuttal would necessitate another article-length piece rather than a letter to the editor, so a few details will have to do. Bloom and Wild quite clearly only use the term *wild* as in *wildly enthusiastic* whilst Scottish Natural Heritage overwhelmingly use *wild* in combinations such as *wildlife* and with no particular reference to wilderness (there is a difference though Silis McCloud [sic] doesn't seem to recognise it). More worrying is the deliberate suppression of parts of a quotation from the RSPB underlined below that suggests the opposite of the facts: 'Loch Druidibeg is a [sic] excellent example of Uist moorland and loch. <u>The area has been managed by crofters for peat cutting and grazing animals.</u> We are managing the area <u>along with the crofters and landowners</u> to benefit the diverse range of wildlife from carnivourous [sic] plants to the mighty sea eagle.'

A patronising and evidence-free critique of the Knepp Estate project contrasts remarkably with a comment from Sir John Lawton, author of the report, 'Making Space for Nature': 'Knepp Estate is one of the most exciting wildlife conservation projects in the UK, and indeed in Europe. If we can bring back nature at this scale and pace just 16 miles from Gatwick airport we can do it anywhere. I've seen it. It's truly wonderful, and it fills me with hope.'

And why shouldn't Brewdog's emphasis be on educating the public when the vast majority of the UK's population is based in urban concentrations which permit little contact and less sympathy with the natural world? This is a widely recognised challenge for conservation.

Mr[s] McCloud [sic] is, however, right that Scotland is not Europe's Last Great Wilderness. How could it be with Lapland and Transylvania in the mix, not to mention Slovenia, which exports its excess brown bears to Italy and Spain for rewilding projects? The ancient Caledonian Forest that covered 15,000 square km following the last ice age is now confined to 180 square km in disconnected pockets of Scotland, so SNH's reforesting aspirations have a long way to go. [S]He is also right that 'we are not in balance [in] the essential relationship between mankind and the world around us', but the imbalance is all on the side of humanity and its ruthless exploitation of the natural world. It was *the hand of man* that cleared the Caledonian Forest. Accounts of explorers in North America describe the teeming abundance of nature such that they were able to run across a river on the backs of the spawning salmon. That has gone but nature has an incredible ability to regenerate itself if left alone and perhaps supplied with a little help. Mr[s] McCleod's [sic] idealistic nostalgia for crofting ignores both the fact that the activity didn't pay enough for his parents not to have to work at other jobs and the fact that the grand estates were no benevolent influence on wildlife, as their records show. To quote from a poem based on those records:

> On Glengarry Estate
> between 1837 and 1840,
> 27 White-tailed Eagles,
> 15 Golden Eagles,
> 18 Ospreys,
> 63 Goshawks,
> 63 Hen Harriers,
> 275 Red Kites,
> 285 Buzzards,
> 462 Kestrels,
> and 198 Wildcats
> were meticulously recorded
> by the gamekeeper who killed them.

This issue is, of course, a fit subject for poetry but 'The Con of the Wild' makes no appropriate connection and I'm left wondering what on earth prompted its publication in a highly respected poetry magazine?

Silis MacLeod writes: I'd like to thank Mr Wynne-Jones for reading my essay on rewilding in Scotland. He has, however, misunderstood much of the argument. I am no apologist for the Scottish shooting estate. In fact, 'The Con of the Wild' is as much a cry to end the irresponsible ownership of vast swathes of the Scottish countryside as much as it is a send-up of the slippery phenomenon of 'wilding'. (Perhaps he misread my passages on the Clearances as a celebration of these acts?) Crofting was always subsistence farming, as in it did not pay. Once the market economy expanded through the Highlands of Scotland, the crofters required money to purchase goods rather than barter between themselves. Many crofters became joiners, gardeners and farmers for the local estate to earn wages. That a lifestyle does not pay a living wage does not mean that it lacks merit or value. Crofting puts people in touch with natural processes and gives them control over their immediate environs as well as their means of consumption. In short, it empowers the human to work with(in) the natural world, rather than against it, as many of our more urban lives do. I do not consider this nostalgic. One can, and does, croft without the presence of 'The Estate'. I trust, however, that Mr Wynne-Jones will forgive my sloppy journalism regarding RSPB Loch Druidibeg, as I excused his frequent misspelling of my name in his letter as well as the erroneous presumption that I must be a man in spite of my published contributor biography. 'The Con of the Wild' was a commissioned article, so he might look to the Gods of Poetry for its relevancy to this highly respected magazine.

News & Notes

The Joan Margarit International Poetry Award • In late July King Philip of Spain launched at the Cervantes Institute, New York, the Joan Margarit International Poetry Award, which will become a key prize on the calendar. Sharon Olds at eighty, with a tremendous haul of awards (Pulitzer, National Book Critics' Circle etc) already on her mantle shelf, is the first recipient. The poet who made a tearful Laura Bush face the human horrors of the Iraq War by publicly rejecting her invitation to the National Book Festival in Washington with a manifesto declaration, herself wept with emotion on receiving it. The purpose of the award was, the King declared, to acknowledge the 'profound personal impact that poetry can produce on its readers'. Note, he used the word *readers* and did not mention *audiences*. Olds translated the eponymous Catalan poet Joan Margarit and was a key advocate of his work. He also translated her. There was something appropriate – 'symmetrical', said one attendee – in that Margarit was returning in spirit the favour of her devotion and skill, and the King was delivering it to her. 'Joan Margarit's work is fierce, and it is partisan', Olds declared when she introduced him to anglophone readers. 'It is on the side of fresh perception. He's a fierce protector of his precise truth, like the bees – like a big bee – with honey. His abstractions and his daily objects are given to the reader with equal, deft, homemade tenderness and brio.'

Two-timing Márquez with Cervantes • Edith Grossman, whose acclaimed translations of *Love in the Time of Cholera* by Gabriel García Márquez and *Don Quixote* by Miguel de Cervantes raised the profile of the often-downplayed role of the translator, died in early autumn, aged eighty-seven. Described as 'an earthy, tough New Yorker who was known as "Edie"', she started translating Latin American and Spanish authors when literary translation was not considered a worthy academic discipline. In her book *Why Translation Matters* (2010), she saw the translator 'not as the weary journeyman of the publishing world, but as a living bridge between two realms of discourse, two realms of experience, and two sets of readers'. Her name was to appear on the cover of any book she translated, alongside that of the author. Her amazing *Don Quixote* was published in 2003 and remains an ineradicable achievement. She also held out for adequate remuneration for translators. A translator was, in her view, engaged in creative activity, and the ear played a key role. 'I think of the author's voice and the sound of the text, then of my obligation to hear both as clearly and profoundly as possible,' she declared in *Why Translation Matters*, adding 'and finally of my equally pressing need to speak the voice in a second language.' Her Márquez sounds very different from her Cervantes. It is not merely a matter of period and country. It has to do with the different dynamics of their imaginations, their tones, their imagined and actual readerships. She also found the voices of Isabel Allende, Carlos Fuentes and Laura Esquivel.

Edith Grossman translated *Don Quixote* over two years, loving every minute. 'Going to the seventeenth century with Cervantes was like going there with Shakespeare, sheer joy.' From the hands of the King of Spain she received the Officer's Cross of the Order of Civil Merit. García Márquez accused her of 'two-timing me with Cervantes'.

Sleeping athletes • Keith Waldrop, who died in late July at the age of ninety, won the National Book Award for poetry in 2009 for *Transcendental Studies: A trilogy*, having first been nominated forty years earlier. He taught at Brown University for four decades and was a celebrated poet, translator (mainly from the French), collagist and, with his wife Rosmarie, a distinguished publisher. In an interview with the radio show 'Close Listening', he remarked that some of his poems came about as his collages did, despite the differences in the creative processes. 'I've never felt that they quite go together, the verbal collages that I do and the visual collages [...] But I enjoy doing both of them, so I do them.' In the early 1960s he founded the magazine *Burning Deck* which he soon co-edited with Rosmarie, turning it into an acclaimed independent publishing house. It started with an old letterpress, bought for $175, which accompanied them on their move from Michigan to Connecticut in 1964. Waldrop started teaching at Brown University. Ben Lerner recalled taking one of his courses. The class was 'composed, on the one hand, of young writers eager to listen to one of the best-read humans on the planet talk about literature, and, on the other, of sleeping athletes who knew Waldrop pretty much gave everybody an A'.

Gboyega Odubanjo • *Lisa Kelly wrote to us*: I am sure you know about the passing of Gboyega Odubanjo, and the impact it has had on the poetry community. He touched so many people and was in such high demand within diverse groups and organisations within the poetry world. Everyone's thoughts are with his family and friends.

It is a very difficult time for the *Magma* team. He has been my Co-Chair since 2020 and joined the board in 2019 when he co-edited the *Act Your Age* issue, going on to co-edit the Obsidian Issue with its focus on Black writers. I wrote a newsletter which I would like to share with you after the *Magma* board met last Friday to mourn and share our grief. We are still reeling.

I had the pleasure of hosting Gboyega at the Torriano Meeting House on Sunday 15 December 2019, and paired him, providentially, with Joe Carrick-Varty. It was their first meeting and they established such a connection that on the way home Joe invited him to co-edit *bath magg*. This is how his presence was felt – people wanted him in their lives, both working and social, for his exceptional poetic skill, talent with people and all-round niceness.

The *Magma* blog contains valuable information about the man and his achievements. 'Everyone he met was touched by his lovely warmth and presence. And everyone who experienced his poetry in performance or through his pamphlets, *While I Yet Live* (Bad Betty Press) and *Aunty Uncle Poems* (Smith/Doorstop Books), which won the 2020 Poetry Business New Poet's Prize, was amazed by his talent, and looking forward to his first full collection, *Adam*, out with Faber next year. Gboyega, as *Magma* Co-Chair, was appreciated for his wise head, his generous outlook, and his positive attitude. [...] It is impossible to comprehend his passing at such a young age – only twenty-seven – but it is possible to carry on his legacy, which we, like many others, will strive to do. His sister, Rose Odubanjo, has set up a fundraiser to establish the Gboyega Odubanjo Foundation for low-income Black writers; at the time of writing, this is well on its way to reaching its £70,000 target which will, no doubt, be exceeded.'

Serious playfulness • *Robert Hampson writes:* The poet Gavin Selerie died in July. He was born in Hampstead in 1949, the son of a wine merchant and recent war-hero. The Selerie family came to London from northern Italy around 1880 and ran a restaurant in Wardour Street. The appreciation of good wine was a family legacy which Gavin happily accepted. Muriel Lee, his mother, worked for a film company in Wardour Street before her marriage and also appeared in advertising films for Spectator Short Films. Her maternal grandfather and uncle, William Henry Grimwood and Herbert Henry Grimwood, were successively principal instructors at the School of Art Wood-Carving, South Kensington.

Gavin Selerie was educated at Haileybury School, and subsequently at Lincoln College, Oxford, and the University of York, where he undertook research on Renaissance literature. He was involved with the counterculture from 1966–76 and in the 1980s was one of the main poetry reviewers for the London listings magazine *City Limits*. His earliest published poetry dates from 1972, and his major books after that are *Azimuth* (1984), *Roxy* (1996), *LeFanu's Ghost* (2006) and *Hariot Double* (2016). He also published *Days of '49* (1999) with the poet and visual artist Alan Halsey (1949–2022). They had first met in the late 1970s and they regularly collaborated thereafter: Halsey produced the cover and section plates for *Azimuth*; they collaborated with David Annwn and others on *Danse Macabre* (1997) and *The Canting Academy* (2008); and Halsey had a graphic input into *Hariot Double*. Selerie favoured long forms, volume-length sequences conceived of as research projects, where original academic research was combined with formal inventiveness and a serious playfulness. *LeFanu's Ghost* was based on research into the complicated Sheridan and LeFanu families, while *Hariot Double* brought together Gavin's

wide-ranging knowledge of the Renaissance, his love of music and his fascination with London by juxtaposing the Renaissance polymath Thomas Hariot and the jazz saxophonist Joe Harriott. Thomas Hariot was a mathematician and astronomer who travelled with Walter Raleigh to the New World; Joe Harriott travelled the other way – from Kingston, Jamaica, to the London jazz scene of the 1950s and 1960s. There were also shorter sequences such as *Elizabethan Overhang* (1989) and *Tilting Square* (1992), and his *Collected Sonnets* were published by Shearsman in 2019. Between 1979 and 1983, Selerie conducted the *Riverside Interviews*, a series of book-length interviews with poets and playwrights (from Allen Ginsberg and Jerome Rothenberg through to Tom McGrath). He published critical work on poetry, beginning with a study of Charles Olson in 1980, as well as two interviews with Ed Dorn (2013) and essays on Pound and contemporary poetry.

Tobias Hill • Just as this issue of *PN Review* was going to press we learned of the death on 26 August of Tobias Hill, at the age of fifty-three. His agent Victoria Hobbs at A.M. Heath said, 'The precision of the poetry fed the prose in a deeply satisfying way'. Latterly he was more celebrated for his prose than his poems, especially *The Love of Stones*, described by his editor Paul Baggaley as 'a wonderful novel which followed the story of a legendary jewel across continents and centuries, and genres, and was typical of his fiction as a whole – atmospheric, dexterous and always engaged with the world and its secrets'. Twenty years ago, his future as a poet seemed assured. In 2004 he was selected as one of the country's Next Generation poets and shortlisted for the *Sunday Times* Young Writer of the Year. He won an Eric Gregory Award in 1995.

Writing from Wales • Carole Strachan has been named Seren Publisher's new chief executive following the retirement of long-term publisher Mick Felton. Seren means 'star' in Welsh. It is a leading independent publishing house specialising in English-language writing from Wales. The press was founded by Cary Archard in 1981. Strachan's experience with the National Trust and other charities, and her work in theatre and music, most recently as chief executive of the contemporary opera company, Music Theatre Wales, make her an unusually suitable candidate. She is also a published writer, her third novel due from Cinnamon Press in 2024. Strachan's appointment, Seren said, 'marks the beginning of an exciting new phase for Seren. Under her leadership, we will continue to champion writers and books from Wales, while also exploring new opportunities for the business'.

Reports

Letter from Finland

ANTHONY VAHNI CAPILDEO

The invitation to Runokuu could not have been more beautiful. Runokuu, 'Poetry Moon', is the fabled and fearless Moon festival of literature, art, music, discussions and unclassifiable invention, which takes place in late summer in Helsinki, Finland. Runokuu's aim is stated openly: to foreground 'experimental, marginal and young poets and poetics', while honouring 'roots and traditions' and inviting international performers to '[broaden] the perspectives of Finnish poetry', creating 'lasting bonds between poetry scenes all around the world'. Quiet yet determined and effective actions – not just gestures – towards the free circulation of ideas characterized the festival. Small booklets, bound in moonlight-grey, were made available free to attendees. These contained samples of the work of poets at the festival, in bilingual and trilingual versions, specially translated for the occasion. The festival follows a safer spaces policy, and there was no alcohol in the green room, but an array of ever-renewed treats and healthy snacks (it is entirely my fault if I ate myself sick on lemon liquorice instead of having a proper meal).

Each year there is a theme. For the nineteenth iteration, in 2023, that theme was 'connection'. Events had begun on the last Thursday in August, with a Poetry Jam, the day before I arrived. The programme's late-night club feeling was cool, rather than cringe; historically grounded, simply there, not self-conscious or try-hard. For the rather amazing venue (sadly, soon to be repurposed by the city council, from what I understand) is Tiivistämö, an 'urban venue that plays host to a range of different events, from concerts to raves, dance competitions and trade fairs', located in the site of the former Suvilhati gas plant, which closed in the 1980s. Clear spaces, circular towers and industrial architecture, black, brick-red, white and metallic, surrounded and led you to the Poetry Moon venues, their indoor stage lighting often in gentle purple. Outdoors, the air was jumping. Across the way was a skate park, built by the skaters who wanted to use it. The feeling was of a common place, angelically alive.

It is my strong desire that places be accessible by water, and timetables reconfigured to allow for travel by river and sea. Until that day comes, there are the aeroplanes, looking so uplifting, while burning our hope of continued breath on this earth. The aeroplane that carried me to Finland was scheduled to arrive just a little too late for me to take up an invitation that promised to connect us, as fellow creatures, to the weird mix of elements that we inhabit. 'If interested in wading in the water, participants are kindly asked to bring their own rubber boots or similar shoes for wading purposes.' As I made my way through the airport, I thought of Milka Luhtaniemi and Matias Loikala, asking people to 'experience surface and matter by wading in them': Luhtaniemi's bilingual lyric essay 'Kantaa, kahlata' ('To Carry, To Wade'; translated by Loikala) was the ground for this happening. The author says: 'I amuse myself with the thought that instead of writing in *a poetic space* I would write at a poetic bottom. At the bottom of the forest and the swamp, in the snow's sense of sink, the catkin, the sprout, the rhizome.' What they hoped for was a communal, yet individual – human, yet emplaced – dance of yielding and resistance: it could be an image of the process of translation, as something living. Like Sophie Collins's image of translation as intimacy, which is more close-up but begins our rethinking of translation as relational, embodied, risky and ethical, this is a more generative approach than the old images of shine-through (meaning imperfection), and fidelity (meaning limit).

I am tempted to pass over details of the travel. We all know the stories by travellers who visit a place utterly unknown to them, for perhaps two days or two weeks, and then make their fame and fortune by issuing generalizations about that place and its people, whose language the traveller seldom speaks. 'I met a fellow whose bearing seemed to me to convey the ancient nobility that runs in the blood of these folk. As he queued for fried chicken at the Pretty Boy Wingery, it struck me how sadly estranged Englishmen have become from their natural et cetera.' Thankfully, I have not inherited eighteenth-century western privilege, and must spare you such pronouncements. I shall say – as a sufferer with complex post-traumatic stress disorder, partly caused by years of microaggressions – Helsinki was one of the kindest, smoothest destinations I have ever been sent to be a poet among poets. When we asked what we might do during our down time, we kept being advised of nearby islands; though I did not make it to any of them, islands with historic houses, islands with protected forest, all sorts of islands just over the way populated the edge of my imagination of where we stood in the city.

Slight slippage of translation might occur in the near-perfect English: 'You can help yourself to juice from the fridge'. I stood confused, then someone not working for the café darted up, showed me the machine cold-pressing fresh ginger and lemon juice (the 'fridge'), and darted away again, before I could thank them. That tact, the darting-away, the quick fix followed by the safe silence, was incredibly soothing and, for me at least, characteristic of my interactions with strangers over the weekend. Finland is a society of engineers. Google Maps – which, when I am triggered, or tired, or dissociating for any reason, can look like a hostile set of blue worms and spinning lines – worked like a dream. At road crossings, cars and cyclists slowed down with unostentatious patience for walkers; no screeching of brakes, inattention, heckling or cursing. I chose to walk forty-five minutes to my first event, confident in the tech, and able to enjoy myself humanly. By blessed coincidence, I also was so fortunate as to attend, in Helsinki Cathedral, the solemn profession of Brother Gregorius as a cooperator brother in the Dominican Order of Preachers. The Ordo Prædicatorum (affectionately, Hounds of the Lord; Domini-canes) were active in Finland in the thirteenth century, but returned only in 1949. Brother Gregorius was the first religious professed in Finland since the Reformation. The Mass was held in Finnish, with some French and Latin. I found myself moved to sing even the syllables I did not understand; a shared celebration taking shape in the air.

I would recommend that you seek out future festivals in person, and details of past programmes; no summary could do justice to the connections made by being alongside other translators and poets from so many places and languages, on walks and at meals, though not (in my case) in the famous sauna... The image I need to leave you with is of my co-performer, Ásta Fanney Sigurðardóttir from Iceland. She recited some poems; interpreted others wordlessly, through motion, though we had the words (in three languages), with an intensity and ferocious grace that reminded me of Bhanu Kapil; finally, she cued the sound and light team. What next? A faint moan began to pick up into a howling. A recorded Icelandic winter, complete with blizzard projection, took over the stage, and our skulls. Ásta turned part wind, part wolf. If unseen wading between land and water became my enduring image for processes of translation, Ásta, lit like an Akira Kurosawa dream, has become my enduring image of more-than-human poetry in the anthropocene.

The National Museum of Taiwan Literature

SHENGCHI HSU

The National Museum of Taiwan Literature (NMTL), founded in 2003 in the city of Tainan, is Taiwan's designated organisation to promote the literary arts on the island.

The museum is set in the grand historic building that originally housed the Tainan Prefectural Government. It was completed in 1916. Like many Meiji-era architects, the celebrated Japanese architect Moriyama Matsunosuke drew on European revivalist style in his design. The building was damaged during the Second World War and suffered decades of neglect. It was not until 1997 that restoration work began. Reopened in 2003, the building is now a focal point of literary culture and activity. It is also a fine example of successful revitalisation of Taiwan's historical buildings.

The NMTL collects, organises and interprets Taiwan's rich literary heritage. Archives and displays reflect the diverse ethnicities of the island. They also chronicle Taiwan's history, ranging from the Dutch colonial period, through the Chinese Ming/Koxinga and Qing dynasties, to the Japanese colonisation and the complex twenty-first century. With a view to promoting awareness of Taiwan's literary arts, the museum devotes much of its energy to education. It regularly holds themed educational events and activities – talks, conferences, interactive exhibitions – to increase awareness of Taiwan's literary traditions. As an exhibition and education venue, the museum also provides family-friendly reading facilities, including a reading room that enhances the literary experience.

The NMTL also works in close association with schools and educational institutions across all levels and throughout the country to promote literature. The museum's website is an interactive multimedia hub which brings together a wealth of searchable literary resources that are accessible and scholarly. As an outreach and widening participation initiative, the NMTL has launched the innovative 'Literature in a Mobile Exhibition Trunk' and 'Equal Opportunities Kit' projects. Theme-based literary exhibition materials are made available on short loans to communities and institutions to set up in public spaces outside the museum.

As well as Taiwan's literary arts, the NMTL also promotes Taiwan's literary heritage. The Taiwan Literature Translation Centre (TLTC) was opened in 2012, aiming to connect Taiwan to the world through literature in translation, which it does through international literary exchanges and collaboration. Publications include anthologies of lesser-known literatures with literary merit and historical significance, thus introducing a diverse range of literature from Taiwan to an international readership. The intention is that readers should gain insight into Taiwan's history and culture through literature. In just a decade, the Centre has established itself as a platform for researchers and scholars of literary translation, as well as for practicing and emerging literary translators. On top of this, the Literature-in-Translation Repository at the Centre collects and consolidates searchable information of literary translation and translators of Taiwan's literary work world-wide.

In helping to spread literary knowledge, the museum intends to make reading and learning literary arts a 'friend for life' through creativity and innovation. From offline research programmes to online information platforms, Taiwan is tapping the power of literary arts and translation to create new resources at home and abroad, ensuring that its unique voices and perspectives are acknowledged around the world.

In 2020, the National Museum of Taiwan Literature began collaborating with the US-based Cambria Press to publish translations of literary works from Taiwan in the 'Literature from Taiwan Series', to showcase the diverse voices from the island. Texts of literary and socio-political significance drawn from Taiwan's long history are selected to offer insights into the country and its culture. For details, visit https://www.cambriapress.com/taiwan-lit.cfm.

A Stone for Daniel Pearl

JONATHAN E. HIRSCHFELD

Credit: © Tom Bonner

The inauguration of the Rabin Peace Memorial at UCLA Hillel in Los Angeles in 2004 was a solemn celebration and the path to the unveiling long and difficult. A few years earlier, living in Jerusalem, I had been contacted with regard to a commission for a sculpture to honour Yitzhak Rabin, the Prime Minister of Israel, assassinated in 1995, barely eight years before. Few murders have had such far-reaching repercussions. I wrote at the time: 'Unlike war memorials, the Rabin Peace Memorial does not recall historical events. It honours the ideal of reciprocity and justice in our relations with others. The rendering of the figures in sunken relief is an acknowledgement of the second commandment. The events in the life of Yitzhak Rabin which inspired this work remind us of how difficult it can be to distinguish illusion from reality.'

After the unveiling, a small elderly couple waited patiently as I spoke with the other guests. I had never seen them before and when they finally approached it felt as if something unexpected was coming. As they glanced up at the dark fossil-like figures that hung over the entrance to the building, they expressed their hope that I might be able to help them. 'My name is Judea Pearl and this is my wife Ruth – we are the parents of Daniel Pearl... perhaps you have heard of us? Have you ever made anything for a cemetery?'

I have no words to describe what my feelings were as I absorbed their presence. Their son, a young American journalist, had been kidnapped and decapitated in Pakistan. Al-Qaeda then broadcast a gruesome video throughout the world as anti-Zionist and anti-American propaganda. The media had been filled with shock, dismay and endless speculation. The French author Bernard-Henri Levy had published the book *Who Killed Daniel Pearl?* and Mariane Pearl, Daniel Pearl's widow, had published *A Mighty Heart*. I had read both.

Their request, on the surface, seemed simple: that I create something to mark the resting place of Daniel Pearl. I learned that he had been buried over two years before, at the Mount Sinai Cemetery, ten miles away. Within a few days of our meeting, Judea Pearl invited me and my wife to join him there. Under an intense blue sky, we found the Mount Sinai Cemetery reminiscent of parts of Israel, simple and austere, although the carefully manicured lawns did reminded us this was indeed southern California. The graves were all marked by bronze or stone plaques flat on the ground. I was struck by the innocence of the place – no trace of history or violence, no broken stones, nothing like the old Jewish cemeteries of Europe. There were few tangible forms of remembrance, apart from inscriptions. Given the circumstances the cemetery director had granted the Pearl family special permission to honour their son on a stone wall adjacent to the plot where he was buried. As we approached the site, we noticed a small temporary label stuck on the ground. I felt an overwhelming emptiness and solitude, and understood the reason I had been brought here.

After our visit we returned to the Pearls' home and over tea, they began to share everything they could about their son. Family photos, videos, published articles, memories of those to whom he had been dear – everything to bring me close to Danny, as they always called him. He was a fine journalist, unafraid to explore a conflicted world, and a talented violinist. He was on the cusp of a new life as a father. They conveyed all this with love and even humour. Their sorrow was bitter and palpable, but never on display.

The Pearls had poured their energies into the Daniel Pearl Foundation, trying by every means to honour their son's memory through the things he valued. Thus an annual world-wide music festival was launched, and a programme to bring journalists from developing countries for apprenticeships in America. Judea Pearl engaged in public, bridge-building dialogues with Akbar Ahmed, a leading authority on contemporary Islam. The Pearls published two books with titles that spoke for themselves – *At Home In the World*, a collection of Daniel's *Wall Street Journal* articles and another, *I Am Jewish* – Daniel Pearl's last words – a collection of short essays from a large range of public figures. Every year renowned journalists and public intellectuals would give lectures in his honour at UCLA and Stanford.

Any sculpture I might imagine would have to be about three by two feet and would be placed on the wall perpendicular to the grave. I was told it could be made of granite or marble, and I knew from the start that I would choose granite. Another stone would lie flat on the ground and would carry text. I was honoured by their request, but within I felt troubled – I had no idea what I could possibly do to relieve the atmosphere of profound sadness that enveloped me as I stood there by that empty place knowing what we all knew. It felt like there was nothing to say, or do, except to bow one's head.

They always referred to him as Danny and it was contagious. I began to feel I knew him, and I would find myself wandering cemeteries looking towards the sky seeking guidance from him. I wanted to find a way to eclipse the morbidity, to shift the experience of this place, to somehow move the mind to another plane. At one point I was at a loss and suggested to Judea and Ruth that we ought to create a memorial at another location. But they were adamant that something was needed here, something beyond words. At one point they suggested that I include a violin and a pen on the wall stone. Nothing so literal, I told them.

In the end the solution came by looking skyward. Dramatic new images of the planet Saturn had recently been published and they suggested vibrations in cosmic space. I began to conceive of a pattern of resonance. The form would evoke music, but it would also embody shock, conveying a sense in abstract terms, of enduring memory and meaning. I produced dozens of patterns, shaping the waves according to some invisible harmony. When I showed them my final rendering there was no doubt I had found it.

Along with a traditional Hebrew text, the ground stone carries the following lines composed by Judea:

Journalist – Musician – Humanist
Lost his life in the pursuit of truth.
In one of the stars
He is still living,
In one of them
He is still laughing:
Perhaps in foreign places
He is still lighting the path of our world.

Originally I had not imagined an inscription on the wall relief. However we live at a time when even a cemetery can feel ephemeral. It was important that the stone always recall Danny, wherever in the course of time it might be found. His parents asked to have inscribed, in Hebrew, *Nigunnim for Danny* – Melodies for Danny.

Incorrigibly Plural

MacNeice and Mahon, Regret and Renewal

M.C. CASELEY

When I started teaching, my first Head of Department was a friendly but authoritative character, who would stand no nonsense from anyone: it made little difference to him whether his antagonist was a quaking, recalcitrant twelve-year-old waster or his own Headmaster. In fact, I soon heard stories of conflict with the latter, of confrontations which allegedly led to desks being violently pounded behind office doors. It gave his detachment and his reputation more lustre: his authority was unquestioned by his colleagues. He could finish a *Times* crossword during a fifteen-minute break; he could throw a crumpled essay back, annotated with salty insults; he could plumb character unerringly in a moment. He was exactly the sort of boss I hoped for, a legendary figure amongst his own fellow teachers, due to his invisibility: he was rarely spotted in the common room, and I suspect beneath it all, he was shy, if not retiring.

Every time I return to the poetry of Louis MacNeice, I give a thought to him because one day, coming across me reading, he growled something about what a wonderful poem 'Snow' was, and drew my attention to it. It has remained with me, because 'Snow' *is* a wonderful poem, a brief, philosophically complex meditation which, in twelve lines, hints and suggests vast vistas to the reader in a seemingly careless, conversational manner. A handful of images in the poem act as shorthand to suggest the complexity of MacNeice's vision as he sits in a lounge and (rather wonderfully) eats a tangerine.

Making my hesitant way through the aftermath of personal grief, I recently read *The Heart of Things: On Memory and Lament* by Richard Holloway, former Bishop of Edinburgh. A brief book, it strings together some of his favourite poems and passages on these topics, together with an elegant, thoughtful commentary: it is full of 'other men's flowers', in Montaigne's phrase, as Holloway candidly admits in the introduction. 'Snow' is one of the poems he considers, alongside one or two other pieces by MacNeice. To Holloway, it illustrates the complexity and plurality of life, an antidote to reductive 'philosophical' poems, because it sprawls on the margins of interpretation, rather than offering a tidying-away of querulous feelings.

In each of the three stanzas of 'Snow', a brief interior is sketched. In the first, the poet is indoors, watching through a bay-window as snow suddenly falls. The transformation is reflected in, and contrasted by, the pink roses set in the window and, observing this, MacNeice notes that the world is 'soundlessly collateral and incompatible': there is a connection between the weather outside and the colours inside – they are somehow parallel, but do not seem to be related. My OED definition of 'collateral' suggests that it describes something coming 'from the same source' and therefore connected, but somehow separate. For MacNeice, the sudden soundless transformation illuminates the plurality of everything he is experiencing: in his unforgettable, casual conclusion halfway through the poem, it is 'incorrigibly plural'. Introducing himself, using the first person, MacNeice commentates on this realisation and, separating the segments of a tangerine, he illustrates it and is intoxicated by the sudden epiphany of 'things being various'. Holloway sees this as an invitation to openness and the rejection of narrow ideological zeal: the poem offers observations which are merely a kind of starting point. 'World is other and other, world is here and there', as MacNeice restates in the later poem 'Plurality'.

It is perhaps the element of surprise that continues to delight readers of 'Snow', as Holloway suggests. The final stanza introduces further sensory images in a rush, only to conclude by reinforcing the collateral nature of both the roses and the snow. The world, as seen by MacNeice, however, is not toothless and merely beautiful: the nature of fire, consuming and flaming in the warm room, reminds the reader that it is also 'spiteful and gay' – both vivacious and destructive. Experiencing the crazy, plural nature of the world is not without cost or danger, as with all intoxication, but the careful qualification of 'incorrigibly' reminds those who would talk lightly of such matters that it is not 'capable of correction', as the OED once

again clarifies. Trying to walk lightly through the world, one sooner or later realises that 'world is other and other' – crazy, spiteful, unpredictable and undeniably plural.

I find Holloway's reading of the poem helpful and, a few pages later in *The Heart of Things*, he follows it with Derek Mahon's fine elegy for MacNeice, 'In Carrowdore Churchyard', in which the 'fragile, solving ambiguity' of 'Snow' is again highlighted. Whereas he characterises Mahon as a 'master of regret', his MacNeice elegy seems, to me, to be more about renewal and celebration, raising the earlier poet from his untimely death from pneumonia contracted while recording a BBC radio feature. The ambiguity which somehow resolves without actually *answering*, seems to be crucial to many MacNeice poems. In 'Entirely', for example, dating from 1940, a similar sequence of sensory experiences posits the idea that all we can do is acknowledge them and embrace partial knowledge. 'If the world were black and white entirely', it would be a different matter, but our 'charts' illustrate whirling chaos rather than clarity, 'a mad weir of tigerish waters' – again the insistence that danger is part of the deal. The conclusion of this poem, however, suggests that clarity, if it were to be provided, may come arm-in-arm with boredom. Even at the very end of his life, MacNeice was still exploring similar ideas: the 1962 'Greyness is all', though a much lesser poem than 'Snow', still suggested that a more neutral grey was more likely to be encountered than the simplistic clarities of black or white, which remained incompatible.

'Snow' is a much earlier poem, dating from 1935, and it's the joyful nature of the epiphany which Holloway omits, despite his appreciation of it as a beautiful artefact of MacNeice's intellectual attitudes. For me, the joy in the sudden apprehension as the snow is suddenly evident is reflected in the witty internal rhyme of 'collateral' and 'incompatible', despite the open contradiction. The sudden shift into the present tense brings the reader closer to the lived experience and the slightly slangy, colloquial tone butts up against more sophisticated, detached judgements about the nature of the world. In doing this, there is a friction generated which suggests the world apprehended is *both/and* rather than the watertight, dogmatic compartments of *either/or*. The world cannot be divided into peel, fruit and pips, unlike the tangerine – there is 'more of it than we think' and all our senses must be brought into play if we are to make any kind of provisional judgements about the relationship between the snow and the roses. The descriptive words MacNeice uses for how the world is encountered – we 'fancy' and 'suppose' things about it – make it clear that only approximate judgements can be made.

My old Head of Department was anything but approximate. His judgements were definitive and clearly expressed, regardless of who was receiving them. He found in MacNeice's poetry, however, a lyrical beauty worth celebrating. Another of his favourites, 'The Sunlight on the Garden', also from the 1930s, dramatises a similar attitude to 'Snow', but is more Shakespearean, with a dying fall. Nevertheless, in this, time is fleeting, life is tragic, mortality certain and only gratitude for the thunder, the rain and the sunlight, ultimately stand. It is a saving grace: the sensory experiences, like those in 'Snow', have value in and of themselves. Grief takes us into uncharted territories; the 'incorrigibly plural' world, however, necessitates that we travel ready for whatever the 'tigerish waters' may throw up, but prepared also to respond to the snow and the roses, and the relationship between them. Any more singular vision we suppose or impose will prove too neat, empty and hollow to be of any lasting consolation in a place where 'world is other and other'.

The Short Poem: a short note

MIKE FREEMAN

In his 354th dreamsong John Berryman wanted poets – maybe readers too – to be protected from long poems. *Vivat* the short poem, but what does that definite article denote? Is *the short poem* merely an indexer's term for all and any poem that turns out to be not long, however short the piece of string may be? Or does it label some sub-genre with recognised and recurring formalities? Are there any structural characteristics that link forms as dissimilar as a sonnet, villanelle, haiku, landau or those short poems which are said to have their own moment 'organically', whatever that may be made to mean?

Perhaps *the short poem* is like Wittgenstein's world: it's whatever is the case. Or, *pace* Wittgenstein again, we might discern a family resemblance amongst the sheer heterogeneity rather than settling cheerfully for a polymorphous perversity. Once, that is, you get beyond the plainest feature: on the page a vertically short block of type jutting out from a horizontally surrounding blankness. As Empson in his own short poem 'Let it go' didn't mean: 'It is this deep blankness is the real thing strange', though that was his poem about giving up on poetry, short or long.

To chew such cud, take three short poems from collections published in 2022 by Carcanet Press: from Alison Brackenbury's *Thorpeness*, Jeffrey Wainwright's *As Best We Can* and Les Murray's final collection *Continuous Creation*. Apart from their shared publisher, this is a random trio as a falsifiability-zone for any putative attribution of a sub-genre.

Alison Brackenbury's 'Lincolnshire Water' in full reads:

Here is strong land, whose grass
does not spill foaming milk,
where I still hear, in February,
taps hiss cold silk.

The single sentence doesn't have time to settle down after the 'Here' pushes forward like the Old English opening *hwæt,* pulling in the reader for the space-time available. It's busily unsettled. The emphatic 'strong' is left open to mean resilient or unforgiving or hard-to-work, followed by what is *dis*allowed. In the turnings and stitchings – here/hear, spill/still, milk/silk – you feel there might be a 'but' coming to start the third line, where it could be *every* or *this* February, with the 'still' as *even now* and *nevertheless.* Not least the last line stays unsettled: syntactically closing a subject-cum-predicate clause, it also reads like a burst – or a 'spill' – of abrupt monosyllabic nouns. Milk isn't spilled, so needn't be cried over, but February's taps pour out a tactile coldness. There's even a gnomic touch, an echo of an Old English riddle: 'Here am I... so what am I?' As it is, the felt moment broadens out in its agro-eco underpinning, the quatrain swinging between negation and affirmation, the poem catching the feeling of being caught in a moment's luminosity – which may be one characteristic of a short poem: a movement through an unsettled but luminous moment.

Les Murray's 'Husbandry' is very different in tone and pace, buttonholing the reader:

You cannot drink bread
you can't butter beer
and it takes at least two men
to plough with a spear –
yet here we are
yet we've got here.

The 'you' of some old adage becomes a bracing 'we' in surviving against the historical 'yet... yet' odds. As there's no buttering beer, fine words butter no parsnips, so fine words are dispensed with in this blunt tone, buttressed by the triple rhyme and the would-you-believe-it close. Its brevity touches on a breadth of history, not so much swords into ploughshares as hunter-gatherers into agrarian communities. My spelling it out like this sounds, tediously, like making a mountain out of a molehill, but it's a *multum in parvo* poem.

A similarity between these two poems is that they have to establish their tone early on, companionably enough before the speaker can get the last word. In the one the reader is left with a multiple, inclusive image; in the other with an affirmation to get over our existential *Angst.* If many a poem [*pace* Empson again] turns on an unresolved conflict, in these two poems the tension reaches a resolution of sorts, even abruptly, almost an epiphany. A luminous moment again?

The third poem, Jeffrey Wainwright's 'This Window Again', doesn't allow an affirmation, much less an epiphany.

I'm looking out of this window again.
There is a cabbage pot-plant
hunkering down for winter, other pots
are empty, rummaged by squirrels.
The trees are starting to bear the marks
or scars, of autumn and I am up against
meaning once more – is there something
out there on the lawn or am I bound
to make up whatever I will believe
is to be found in a tree or season?

Instead of epiphany the window opens up on – *absit omen* – the epistemological aporia, with the poem itself a tentative facet of what's being queried. The moment isn't one of luminosity, other than of facing what's at stake. The first half is grounded in a texture of conversational and concrete diction – so no comfort of a pathetic fallacy or mystifying an image – then the shift to direct conjecturing, where 'bound to' is both a limitation and an inescapability. As for 'something out there' it's more likely we have to 'make [it] up', to quote the title of his 2020 collection, *As Best We Can*, teasing our meanings from 'a tree or season', where 'season' disallows the lurking rhyme with 'reason'. Perhaps there's a meta-statement: framing such a question in a poem like this is at least one way of coping with the question. That there isn't a ready luminosity to be had is the moment that's being moved through.

Each of these poems engages the reader in a different sort of conversation, but a commonality is that they don't close each door they open. 'Still' and 'here' and 'whatever' leave their spaces; their brevity isn't lapidary; even the Murray is so insistent that, contrariwise, you can't resist a 'well, so far, anyway...'. They're short but they don't stop short, each turns on a moment of reflection: the first is grounded in and grows through its imagery, the second muscles in on aphorisms, the third pushes 'up against' the unreliable – but perhaps the only available – ways and means. Berryman's Henry – himself a leaf out of Whitman's *Leaves* – might acknowledge that some short poems are large, they contain multitudes.

Yet two other features deserve a nod. One plain fact about a short poem is that its very shortness lets you hold in your mind, even in your line of sight, the beginning that you've just left, even 'in my end is my beginning'. It's likely to echo more loudly, the *gestalt* sitting more squarely. And this is to raise the whole phenomenology of reading rather than offering an excursion into genre-theory. A further route is signalled in an earlier (2002) collection of short poems by Les Murray entitled *Poems the Size of Photographs.* Perhaps there's a verbal correlative with the visual form; structural homologies beckon. A photographic image isn't an instant blink: as in a short poem, your attention is engaged to move through the image, its texture and structure. But Murray's poem 'A Dog's Bad Name' – albeit chuntering about his politics – might apply to categorising his short poems: 'I never know their outlines in advance; / all I know is no group makes them'.

Enough already. Whatever tentative commonalities have been touched on here, it seems neither necessary nor at all sufficient to postulate some generic paradigm. That would be to short-change short poems. Some subgenre taxonomy wouldn't offer much to Berryman by way of a toy or dream or rest, or help Murray in *Killing the Black Dog.* Maybe we should give such hypostatising short shrift, settling for *this* short poems and *that* short poem, not *the short poem.*

Letter from Wales

SAM ADAMS

Un funud fach cyn elo'r haul o'r wybren,
Un funud fwyn cyn delo'r hwyr i'w hynt,
I gofio am y pethau angofiedig
Ar goll yn awr yn llwch yr amser gynt.

Read aloud, the opening stanza of 'Cofio', a relatively early poem by Waldo Williams (everywhere known and referred to as 'Waldo'), has hypnotic power. Even without the ability to read the lines, far less understand them, such is the consistency of letter sounds in Welsh that, if you look attentively, you can *see* its music, a notation that is anciently a vital part of Welsh prosody.

The poet was born in September 1904 in Haverfordwest, south Pembrokeshire. That 'south' is significant, because historically it is an English-speaking area. Furthermore, his mother, Angharad, born in Shropshire, spoke only English, so that became 'the language of the hearth' as the Welsh saying has it. She was, however, of a remarkable Flintshire family: her paternal uncle was Sir Henry Jones (1852–1922), a cobbler's son who left school at twelve but, largely self-taught initially, went on to become Professor of Moral Philosophy at Glasgow University. For Waldo, however, all changed when, in 1911, his Welsh-speaking father, Edwal, was appointed headmaster of the primary school at Mynachlogddu, and brought the family to the foothills of Preseli, north of the *landsker,* that notional dividing line across the county, where Welsh is still the common language of everyday use. In a 'Writers of Wales' book, his close friend, the late James Nicholas (a sometime colleague I knew as 'Jâms', himself a poet of distinction and Archdruid of the Gorsedd of Bards in the 1980s), says Waldo learned Welsh in Mynachlogddu as a seven-year-old, from his playfellows.

Following grammar school education at Narbeth, which entailed lodging in that small town during the week, Waldo proceeded to UCW Aberystwyth (1923–7) where he read English and found deep and lasting pleasure in the poetry of the Romantic period. In his final year he edited the college magazine. Jâms's book includes a characteristically light-hearted essay on 'Digs' published that year in *The Dragon*, in which Waldo describes friendly games of 'Ping-Pong… played under rules which vary with the size of the table, and whether the cracks in it are longitudinal or latitudinal'. (And I would wager the 'net' was a row of prescribed texts, aligned spines uppermost across the middle, for we did precisely the same in Aber digs in the 1950s, even to the cracked table-top hazard.) In digs he also became friendly with Idwal Jones, a schoolteacher who stayed at weekends and with whom he fell into a routine of composing parodic and satirical verses. Similar close friendships largely based on a shared interest in reading and writing poetry became an influential feature of his life.

From Aber, Waldo embarked on a career in Pembrokeshire primary schools, for much of the time as a supply teacher. Out of the debris of an incomplete effort originally intended for the Crown competition in the National Eisteddfod held at Liverpool in 1929, or in Jâms's version of events, for a local eisteddfod at Clunderwen and inspired by a visit to the farm of a friend, he somehow summoned 'Cofio' (Remembering). It first appeared in the September 1931 number of *Y Ford Gron* (The Round Table), a short-lived Welsh-language monthly published in Wrexham, to which Waldo was a frequent contributor of both light-hearted prose and mostly brief verses in similar vein. 'Cofio' stands out among the best loved of his poems, though we are told Waldo was himself critical of it. What do the Welsh words that begin this 'Letter' mean? Tony Conran's verse translation brings the reader the spirit and something of the music of the original:

Before the sun has left the sky, one minute,
One dear minute, before the journeying night,
To call to mind the things that are forgotten
Now in the dust of ages lost from sight.

Although not a regular competitor for eisteddfod prizes, his long poem in the 'strict metres' on the subject 'Tŷ Dewi' (St Davids) was placed second among entries for the Chair in the National at Abergwaun (Fishguard) in 1936. Earlier the same year, ever a companionable man, he had collaborated with a friend, E. Llwyd Williams, to produce *Cerddi'r Plant*, a book of poems for children, which has retained its charm to the present. It was a shaft of light into encroaching darkness: early in March that year, Europe had been sent reeling by Germany's occupation of the Rhineland. By 1938, preparations for war were advancing and compulsory service in the armed forces was proposed. 'Y Twr a'r Graig' (The Tower and the Rock), another long, strict-metre poem, was Waldo's first response; refusal to participate in the

war effort his second. Although too old for call-up, he registered as a conscientious objector. At a tribunal in February 1942 he said: 'I believe all men to be brothers and to be humble partakers of the Divine Imagination that brought forth the world… War to me is the most monstrous violation of this Spirit… I consider all soldiering to be wrong; for it places other obligations before a man's first duty to his brother.' He was declared unconditionally exempt, but that was not to be the last of his brushes with the State.

In April 1941 Waldo had married Linda Llewellyn, originally from Maerdy in the Rhondda, and now the possibility of notoriety as a 'conchie' drove him from Pembrokeshire to a post in the secondary school at Botwnnog on the Llŷn peninsula. There his wife, diagnosed with TB, died in June 1943. She was, he wrote, 'my inspiration… My strong-hearted one… My heaven, my eternal nest'. Unsettled, he spent the years 1945–9 teaching at schools in England and at Builth Wells in Powys before returning to Pembrokeshire. He was getting by there with supply teaching and extra-mural classes when the Korean War started. That conflict, 1950–3, which cost more than 2.5 million lives, forced him to another stand. He gave up school work where pay was taxed at source and refused to surrender income tax on his extra-mural earnings on the grounds that to do so would be to contribute to the war effort. He maintained this stand until the end of conscription in 1963, despite the seizure of his furniture and possessions and two periods of imprisonment. In the midst of turmoil, he wrote no poetry, but, drawn by its 'doctrine of the inner Light and the practice of silence in the service of worship', in 1953 he became a Quaker.

The poem for which he is instantly remembered, 'Mewn Dau Gae' (In Two Fields), was published in the weekly *Baner ac Amseru Cymru*, 15 February 1956. Later that year it was included in *Dail Pren* (Leaves of the Tree), his only collection of poems. Translated, the title is reminiscent of Whitman's *Leaves of Grass*, whether that was intended we cannot say, but the American was certainly an influence, as was Langland, whose 'field full of folk' in 'Piers Plowman' is echoed in the phrase 'perci llawn pobl' in the final stanza. Waldo had found his true home among the Quakers, whose transcendentalism chimed with the personal experience that underlies this visionary, rapturous utterance, there still in Conran's version:

Am hyn y myfyria'r dydd dan yr haul a'r cwmwl…
Day broods on all this beneath sun and cloud,
And night through the cells of her wide-branching
   brain –
How quiet they are, and she breathing freely
Over Flower Meadow Field and Flower Field –
Keeps a grip on their object, a field full of folk.
Surely these things must come. What hour will it be
That the outlaw comes, the hunter, the claimant to the
   breach,
That the Exiled King cometh, and the rushes part in
   his way?

Siracusa and other new poems

JOACHIM SARTORIUS

Translated by Richard Dove

from Joachim Sartorius, *Wohin mit den Augen. Gedichte*, Cologne 2021

Waking in Ortigia ('Aufwachen in Ortigia')

Night washes the sea.
The water new by dawn.
On the retina light
paid for with white spume.

I brush salt from the table.
I kiss the lizard's eyes.
I cut the bread.
The day's now uncommonly bright.

Later the ocean
relieves you of the coins
and carves
a nymph's name into each

for the long delight
of being alive.

The necropolis of Pantalica ('Die Nekropole von Pantalica')

The crane flies into the forests and fills its wings with spices.
The sky is stretched out bright-grey like a hide.

I am the shepherd, slitting figs.
Speak pretty things about the grey sheep.

And prettier things still about the dark graves.
About the first butterfly, brown and nervous.

High on the mountain lies wide open
the manual charting its modes of flight.

Siracusa ('Siracusa')

Beneath the swartly welling water,
Arethusa, I caught sight of you,
your skin more albine than ricotta
and just as firm as an unripe grape.

Then you were covered by wings and reeds.
I'd lain in wait, behind the aerial roots at the end
of the long vacant avenue, for you.
By the sea that's unalloyed with the source.

The river-god's limp, all creatures wrapped
in summer sleep beneath the sombrest rock overhangs.
Yet everywhere where it is sombre it's written
That I, Arethusa, am searching for you.

At night I see people propping up cafés.
I don't give up. They think I'm far gone
when I call: empathise
with this story of love between two rivers.

Morire a Siracusa ('Morire a Siracusa')

All that I, wandering rhapsodist, could need
Is a good friend, some sweet wine in the shade
And that my name still echoes when I'm dead.
                    (Count August von Platen, 1796–1835)

He flees the cholera, breakneck from Naples down to Palermo.
From Palermo across to Syracuse
where he takes up lodgings in Albergo Aretusa.
Wholly secluded from the world,
as he notes in his diary on 13 Nov 1835.
The youths have no time for this pallid figure.
The strength for summer has drained out of him.
Intestinal bleeding and other infirmities.
The dialect of the sickbed is a secret language.
Words only valid during the night.
Made for the night where they lose themselves.
Graduating to souls. No more ghazals.
Baron Landolina's servant is at a loss.
The count dies, just 39, in his arms
under Magna Graecia's sun.

His grave is hewn into the lesser latomia.
Landolina sees to it, furnishing marble, inscription.
Words outlast graves as they outspeak death.
His fame? It has paled the way he did in his final days.
And yet admirers from Ansbach, his northerly birthplace,
keep tending his tomb.

Téléphone arabe ('Téléphone arabe')

thinking of Ibn Hamdis

1.

His divan we have twice, set down by himself
in punctilious elated calligraphy.
A copy flirting with dust in the Vatican Library.
The other in the Asiatic Museum in St. Petersburg.
How did they get there? The late poems ponder
the dialectics of ageing. He died on Mallorca in Palma,
after aleatory wanderings, at seventy-seven.

2.

Right to the end his hair was curly and dark-brown.
Yet it seemed to his friends at the court in Seville
a white aura was hovering round his head.
And so he was known as The Hoary One (or The Sprightly and Wise).
In his poems his own decrepitude
got conflated with the decline of the Arab world in Sicily, Andalusia.
He'd fled by ship from Syracuse to Taparura.

3.

Fled when the Normans made land. His ship ran
aground. No-one writes about the loss
of his heart. He writes sweet yearning elegies
on the loss of drowned Javhara. Even now
they line our path like snakeskins.
Téléphone arabe, a crackling message as far as the Balearics,
far from the Vatican, even further from Petersburg.

Porto Grande Syracuse ('Großer Hafen von Syrakus')

When no longer able to glimpse the rays
off the golden shield of Artemis, they threw
honey, incense into the waves.

The honey sank down undiffused to the wrecks
on the sea floor. This is where the Athenian fleet
was locked in battle with Syracuse, a colony

that had grown too mighty and arrogant.
Athens succumbed. One hundred and fifty vessels sank,
the water stained red, so covered with humiliation.

7,000 Athenians, they reckon, were pressed into slavery
and laboured in the latomiae. These quarries today
are green, enchanted, the stuff of scenic snapshots,

the waters of the Porto Grande that witnessed the crassest
of all battles a rippled mirror. Let's raise
a toast to Hermocrates, to Gelon!

As always, though, we rejoiced too soon in their victories.
The Syracusans leapt across blind glass,
expended themselves in petty wars. Unstoppable: Rome.

Exercises: What remains ('Übungen: Was bleibt')

Furious blue back there and ahead of us
greyness. Grey rotundity. Gruffly outsized
the stone seashell of the theatre.
Which housed Sophocles, Aristophanes.
Now lizards are flitting across dry stones.
Sand has set a bound to the sea.

This way almost nothing is left
of the temptation of power. A tiny clutch of anecdotes.
An ant trail. Left to our own devices
we strike out ahead in the midst of the gorge.
The stones are already sporting dark stains.
The sea has been set a bound by sand.

Epitaph of a Phoenician ('Epitaph eines Phöniziers')

Pointless
to approach my stele.
Neither gold nor gems
nothing else of value
was buried with me.
I'm lying here in the clothes
I had on last, deep in the earth
and am falling more and more apart.
I'm lying in the arms of Baal,
in the lap of Edom,
of all the Great Silence's other envoys.
I'd ask you not to destroy this force.

Laboratoire des Marbres ('Laboratoire des Marbres')

The north wind and the sea as unsoiled
as 3,000 years ago when Menelaus
landed at Ras el Tin. Many in Alex
busy themselves with Eternity.
Monsieur Basile Bass for one. He runs
the *Laboratorie des Marbres* in Ramleh.
On the letterhead: marble from, one beneath
the other, Constantinople or Hellas or Italy.
M. Bass is a supplier and sculptor in one.
He purveys monuments, angels and graves
in whatever shape, designing the vault of Hariklia,
the poet's mother, while she was still
hugely alive and getting advances
from Isma'il Pasha, Egypt's viceroy no less. The touch
of her white forearm. Perpetuated
life-long in the curve of the angel's back.

Orlando Fantastico: Il non credibile vero

ALBERTO MANGUEL

Forse era ver, ma non però credibile
OF, Canto I:56

We speak in a hall of dark mirrors. What we put into words seems to conjure up its opposite from the shadows, which in turn echo its own dark reflection. Nothing stands clearly on its own. A definition of fantasy, therefore, implies a definition of what is real, and what is real assumes the knowledge of what is fantasy. For a sixteenth-century Italian, reality is obviously different than for an Italian of our catastrophic times, and perhaps it was no less so for a Spaniard or a Portuguese of the same century. Plato's heavenly spheres were real in the Ptolemaic universe; space travel was a fantasy, allowed only to heroes and magicians and the ancient gods. For us, today's cosmological reality is that of which we dreamed, not so long ago, in our science-fiction stories. In the age of fake news and photoshopping, the distinction between what is real and what is fantasy is even more blurred. The mirrors of perception keep shifting and we are all, at some time or another in our lives, inside Atlante's magical palace of illusions that are, to our conscious senses, real. Reality, as we know, is constructed from what we take to be our personal experience and from the received (and admitted) experience of others. But fantasy, too, employs those same tools. Realty and fantasy, real world and dream world, are in the eye of the beholder. Victor Hugo summed up this notion in *La fin de Satan*: 'I know what Hell fits in the apple of the eye.'[1]

What is real for Orlando also fits in 'the apple of the eye'. The palace of Atlante is merely the summing-up of this conflation of realities, reality conceived and reality perceived. Fantasy is only outside the book, beyond the page, in the eyes of the reader, a shadow born from the reader's preconceptions of reality. Ariosto knowingly defends this paradox:

Although deceit is mostly disapproved,
Seeming to show a mind malevolent,
Many a time it brings, as has been proved,
Advantages that are self-evident.

Certainly, Atlante's palace is the obdurate persistence of deceitful fantasy, but it is also the persistence of reality, the place where the kaleidoscopic nature of the world is fixed in an appearance that freezes desire into fact. In Ariosto's poem, what you imagine you see, what you imagine you desire, is what you get. In this enchanted palace, Orlando sees the fleeting Angelica because he seeks the fleeting Angelica; he sees the valorous knights Ruggiero, Gradasso, Iroldo, Brandimarte and Prasildo, because in his mind they are his rivals. And they in turn see the fleeting Angelica because they too desire to see the fleeting Angelica. However, there are nuances in the appearance of reality. Ruggiero, for instance, hears in the voice that Orlando takes to be that of Angelica calling for help, the voice of his beloved Bradamante[2]. The reality, the fantasy, the text are all one and the same. It is our reading that is individually selective and divisive: in Atlante's palace everyone is Pierre Menard. Only Astolfo will escape the fantasy by sounding the real horn that creates the illusion of terror. The 'so fierce and terrible a sound'[3] is more real than reality itself.

In the reality of Ariosto, a reality dreamed up by the poet who becomes a character in his own fantasy (and therefore a fantasy as well in the logical reality of the poem), there are, among many other real elements, the books in Ariosto's library. After all, Ariosto is a scholar-poet, an illustrated courtier-clerk, a distinguished member of that *umanesimo* for which he invented the much-abused term. In the pages of his books, Ariosto (like his contemporaries) has read things that he deems real and other things that he deems fantasy.

Unless with touch and sight they've plainly proved
A thing, [they] will not believe; thus it comes,
This canto will seem strange to stay-at-homes.[4]

For this distinction between fantasy and reality there are no rules: faith, *auctoritas*, sight and touch, confirmation of personal experience, the word given by others, all these elements colour the descriptions of people and places, of foreign lands and past events depicted in atlases, chronicles, novels of chivalry and epic poems. Much the same is true for the readers of Ariosto's poem: the city of Paris and the emperor Charlemagne are real (though not perhaps as Ariosto presents them); Melissa and Discordia are not (unless we read them as symbols or metaphors, as Galileo proposed in his *Postille all'Ariosto*[5].) To this bipartisan view we must add a third: what

---

2 *OF*, Canto XXII

3 *OF*, Canto XV:15 ['orribil suono']

4 OF, Canto VII:1 ["l sciocco vulgo non gli vuol dar fede, / se non le vede e tocca chiare e piane. / Per questo io so che l'inesperienza / farà al mio canto dar poca credenza.']

5 Galileo Galilei, 'Postille all'Ariosto', in *Scritti letterari*, vol. IX (Milano: Casa editrice Sonzogno, 1933) pp.149–194.

---

1 Victor Hugo, 'Deux différentes manières d'aimer', dans *La fin de Satan* (Paris: G. Charpentier & Cie, Editeurs, 1888) p. 66 ['Je sais ce que l'enfer met dans une prunelle']

is fantastic for us is real for his characters. Astolfo's comprehensive book of spells ('the one that teaches how to undo charms'[6]) is, alas, fantastic for us, his sceptical readers, but assuredly real for Astolfo himself. We, unlike Astolfo, are like poor Orlando deciphering in Arabic calligraphy the names of Angelica and Medoro on the trunks of the forest trees and on the walls of the cave. The signs are real but we long to read them as fantasy.

Ariosto's fantasy begins in the core of the reality of his characters. This is a tangled, convoluted, endlessly complex reality that refuses to follow a straight path but, as in the future world of non-Euclidian geometries, follows several possible paths simultaneously. Almost every time that a conflict threatens to be resolved or a liaison is on the point of being sealed, something or someone intervenes, shattering the wishful coherence of the story into a kaleidoscopic reality that is constantly changing, thus transforming historical time into a nightmare of eternity. Barely a century after Ariosto, in that England clearly marked out in the flight pattern of Ariosto's heroes, Thomas Hobbes, trying to make sense of the reality of his nation shattered by the Civil War, objected to this notion of a bustling but instantaneous eternity, and argued that a 'Standing still of the Present Time, a *Nunc-stans* (as the Schools call it)' cannot be understood by anyone, 'no more than they would a *Hic-stans* for an Infinite greatnesse of Place'.[7] Hobbes seems not to have read *Orlando furioso*, readily available in Sir John Harington's translation of 1591. Because in *Orlando* everything happens as in a sort of narrative eternity, in no one single place or time but in all places and all times. The Past, the Present and the Future are (as today's astrophysics teaches us) simultaneous and yet distinct. The readers need not choose: they can follow all roads at once, as an inquisitive child might do, or wishes he might do. *Orlando furioso* is a Scheherazadian narrative whose progression is not mathematically sequential but geometrically unending.

And yet, Hobbes himself admitted that fantasy can root itself in the ersatz-reality depicted by a poet. 'A man can fancy Shapes he never saw', he wrote, 'as the Poets make their Centaures, Chimeraes, or other Monsters never seen.'[8] Hobbes (condescendingly) admits the poetic reality of a fantastic menagerie, such as the magical mounts that allow the heroes to travel through the entire globe and have a comprehensive *Weltanschauung* at the same time. Rabicano, the horse born from fire and wind, so light on its hoofs that it leaves no trace on either sand nor snow, takes Ruggiero from India to Europe, crossing mountains and seas, across Egypt and crossing Cathay, over the Himalayas, from northern Scythia to the Caspian, and inspecting on his whirlwind tour the Polish, Hungarian and German lands.[9] The Hippogriff goes further and takes Astolfo to the Moon.

The world narrated by Ariosto is polyphonic, the multifarious style forbidden by John XXII in his 1324 bull *Docta Sanctorum Patrum*[10] for being 'frivolous, impious, lascivious and an obstruction to the audibility of the words'. Two centuries later, Ariosto was not troubled by the interdiction. Cardinal Ippolito d'Este, to whose household the young Ariosto was attached and to whom the poet dedicated his *Orlando furioso*, responded to reading it with a humdrum question: 'Master Ludovico, from where did you get all these cock-and-bull stories?'[11] The exuberant narrative profusion of *Orlando furioso* might obscure the fact that Ariosto is, however improbable his fantasy, a poet deeply rooted in material reality, in the cartography, botany, zoology, architecture, dress and weaponry of his characters. His historical chronology follows only poetic logic and is conveniently loose to suit the action – 'if your lofty thoughts bend down a little', he says to the reader, 'to make room among them for my verses'.[12] His psychology, however, seems less keen: everyone in *Orlando furioso* (above all Orlando himself) is driven by a specific passion that sets them into action like a clockwork key: turn the key, start the poem, and they are off, fleeing, pursuing, fighting, always in motion. If there are a few quiet moments in *Orlando*, they are hardly memorable; they seem to be merely there to allow the characters to catch a rare breath. And then we're off again. If *Orlando furioso* is a perfect intertwining of real fantasy and fantastic reality, its braided strands criss-crossing and shifting meaning throughout generations of readers up to our day, then what keeps the whole tapestry present as a whole in the mind of its readers is essentially its vitality, the constant toing and froing, the poem as the breath of life.

Though Ariosto himself travelled to several cities in the Italian peninsula – Mantova, Urbino, Venezia, Bologna, Firenze – his physical universe was essentially constrained to Ferrara. Lina Bolzoni has noted that 'Ariosto the poet travels across maps rather than across land and sea; locked in his room, with the help of atlases, he travels freely, safe from wars and storms; his world, his realms, appear incompatible with the Ptolemaic

6 *OF*, Canto XV:79 [My translation] ['quel ch'agl' incanti riparare insegna']

7 Thomas Hobbes, *Leviathan or the Matter, Forme, & Power of a Common-Wealth Ecclesiastical and Civill* (London: Andrew Crooke, 1651) p. 421

8 Idem, 45, p. 448

9 *OF*, Canto X:71 ['il Cataio, e quindi Mangiana / sopra il gran Quinsaì... l'iperborei Sciti... i Pollacchi, i Ungari, the Germani... e al resto / di quella boreale orrida terra.']

10 'Docta sanctorum patrum' in *Corpus juris canonici emendatum et notis illustratum. Gregorii XIII. pont. max. iussu editum.* (Rome : In aedibus Populi Romani, 1582) 3 parts in 4 volumes, Vol. I, pp. 1256–7.

11 Antonio Cappelli, 'Prefazione storico-critica' in *Lettere di Ludovico Ariosto* (Milano: Ulrico Hoepli, 1887) p. LV ['Messer Ludovico, dove mai avete trovato tante corbellerie?'

12 *OF*, Canto I:4 ['e vostri pensier cedino un poco, / si che tra lor miei versi abbiano loco.']

universe, and seem to expand into infinity'.[13] The metaphor of the library as universe could have been coined for Ariosto: because of his reading, he is everywhere between the pages of his books. With poetic justice, Ariosto died in his Ferrara, supposedly of consumption on 6 July 1533, still correcting the final cantos of his *Orlando furioso*.

Some fifteen hundred miles from Ariosto's deathbed (a distance that the Hippogriff would have crossed in the blink of an eye) a young boy, Luís Vaz de Camões, would have read of the wonderful adventures with a fascination that would last a lifetime. The Camões family, following the royal court, escaped the plague that was threatening Lisbon (Luís's first escape from the dreaded disease) and settled in Coimbra. There, Luís's uncle, a chancellor of the university and the prior of the Monastery of Santa Cruz, took on the boy's education. It was probably in Coimbra that the young Camões came across Ariosto's poem in Jerónimo Jiménez de Urrea's Spanish version of 1549, a translation so popular that it enjoyed eighteen different editions in the sixteenth century alone. Only half a century years later, however, Cervantes, in *Don Quixote*, derided Urrea's effort: he had his priest tell the barber, while they are purging Don Quixote's library, that if he found an edition of Ariosto's *Orlando* in a different language than that of the original, he wouldn't show it the slightest respect, but if it was one that 'speaks in its own tongue, I'll hold it high above my head'.[14] Reading *Orlando furioso* in his youth, Camões would have been thrilled to find among the thousands of lines of verse a mention of his homeland in the unhappy figure of Tesira, king of 'Ulisbona', fighting bravely (if wrongly) on the side of the Pagans before being killed by Rinaldo. In Ariosto's poem, courage and bravery are equal qualities among Christians and Moors. Camões would identify with that sentiment – equal courage between enemies – though he would later refer to the Moors (as opposers of Christianity) as *falsos, astutos, enganosos, malíciosos* and *pérfidos* (false, crafty, deceitful, malicious and perfidious): in short, *gentes infernais* (a hellish race). For Ariosto, the Moors are the collective Other. Only when addressed individually do they become characters with distinct features, like the fierce Rodomonte, who will have the honour of closing the poem as he angrily crosses the Acheron (like Virgil's Turnus) into the Kingdom of the Dead.

Though tradition has it that the young Camões was an undisciplined student, his early work shows a wonderful familiarity with both the ancient classics and the contemporary Italian, French and Spanish authors. Whatever his studies in Coimbra might have been, at the age of twenty or so Camões moved back to Lisbon to complete his schooling and there, in spite of his scarce means, he was admitted at the court of King João III, thanks to the Camões family name that harkened back to Galician nobility[15].

In 1546, Camões's luck turned. He was exiled from Lisbon, perhaps by royal decree for an unspecified crime, and joined the garrison in Ceuta as a common soldier, thereafter losing his left eye in action. He returned to Lisbon, was arrested during a brawl and released only on the promise of enlisting on a ship bound for India. He sailed in 1553 and visited, among other exotic places, the Malabar Coast and the Red Sea. Recalled to Goa after another quarrel, this time on board, he was shipwrecked off the coast of Cambodia before a new sentence could be meted out. The able-bodied Camões was able to save his life by swimming back to shore, clutching (tradition has it) a bundle of newly-written verses in his hand. But once again in Goa, Camões was jailed for debt, and later had to borrow the fare for the voyage home. He reached Lisbon in April 1570, in the midst of yet another plague.

In 1578, during an ill-planned invasion of Morocco, the young King Sebastião was killed with much of the Portuguese nobility, the tragedy giving rise to a national legend that was later claimed by the dictatorial regime of Salazar. On 10 June 1580, Camões died in uttermost poverty, struck down by the plague that had been pursuing him since his childhood. Decades later, what were assumed to be his bones were interred with much pomp in the Monastery of the Jerónimos in Lisbon.

The verses rescued from the shipwreck (the story goes) turned out to be what is recognized as Portugal's national poem, *The Lusiads*. The book was published in 1572, eight years before Camões's death, and earned the poet a small royal pension for 'the adequacy of the book he wrote on Indian matters'.

The Lusiads contains many references to *Orlando furioso*, some overt, some implied, but the two epic poems are notably different. Ariosto constantly manoeuvres the reader between what is fantasy and what is real: what is real for his characters and fantasy for his readers (and perhaps for him.) Camões insists that everything in his poem is real, nothing is fantasy, even the ancient gods. *The Lusiads* is, first and foremost, a new *Aeneid*, the account of the birth not of Rome but of the new empire of Portugal. 'My theme is the daring and renown of the Portuguese, to whom Neptune and Mars alike give homage. The heroes and poets of old have had their day; another and loftier conception of valour has arisen.'[16] And criticizing the epic poets for their fantastical inven-

13 Lina Bolzoni, 'Introduzione' in Lina Bolzoni & Carlo Alberto Girotto, *Donne, cavalieri, incanti, follia: Viaggio attraverso le immagini dell'Orlando furioso* (Lucca: Maria Pacini Fazzi editore, 2012) p. 8 ['Il poeta Ariosto viaggia sulle carte, più che per mare e per terra; chiuso nella sua stanza, aiutandosi con le carte geografiche, viaggia gratuitamente, protetto da guerra e tempeste; il suo mondo, i suoi spazi, sembrano incompatibili con l'universo tolemaico, sembrano dilatarsi all'infinito.']
14 Miguel de Cervantes, *Don Quijote de la Mancha*, Primera Parte, cap. 6 (Madrid: Real Academia Española, 2015) p. 87 ['que habla en otra lengua que la suya, no le guardaré respeto alguno; pero si habla en su idioma, le pondré sobre mi cabeza.']

15 A.J. Saraiva & Óscar Lopes, *História da Literatura Portuguesa*, 17a edição, corregida e actualizada (Porto: Porto editora, 2017) p. 312
16 Luis de Camões, *Os Lusíadas*, Canto I ['Que eu canto o peito ilustre lusitano, / A quem Neptuno e Marte obedeceram. / Cesse tudo o que a Musa antiga canta, / Que outro valor mais alto se alevanta.']

tions, Camões says: 'Well may they deck out their empty fables, mere dream-stuff, with ever new refinements. The story I tell is the truth naked and unadorned and admits no comparison with such, for all their grandiloquence.'[17] Ariosto is not mentioned by name, but for Camões's readers the allusion to 'mere dream-stuff' was clear.

This insistence that the poet's story is real but that other stories are fantasy recalls Dante's device in the *Inferno* when, in order to have the reader believe in his forthcoming description of Geronte, the monster of fraud, Dante says: 'by the lines of this my comedy, reader, I swear.'[18] The fantasy of one fiction (in the poet's own words) is deemed real; the fantasies of others are not so trustworthy. Camões, in spite of being obviously under the influence of Ariosto, wants to distance himself from the multitudinous tangles of the Italian poet by setting the course of his hero, Vasco da Gama, on a straight line in which the factual and documentary simply alternate with the fantasy, the one contaminating the other with their intrinsic qualities: the documented voyage of the Portuguese explorer acquires a mythological grandeur when discussed by the Olympian gods; the Olympian arguments over the destiny of Portugal take on (as with Bacchus' tantrums and Venus' come-hither poses) a very down-to-earth flavour. But while for Ariosto no choice of path need be made because all paths are simultaneously undertaken, for Camões there is only one road from the ambitions of Portugal to the riches of India, and, for his Vasco da Gama, only one life to be lived. It therefore better be the right one.

Ariosto can populate his geographics with all manner of fantastic beasts, objects and events, shifting easily from the realistic description of an armour or a musket to a magic ring or a flying steed. Enchanters, giants, ravenous crocodiles, sea monsters appear without a note of apology, and arbitrary chance has the same prestige as material consequence. In *Orlando furioso* there's something happening all the time, whether fantastic or historically sound, because life, for Ariosto, is a galaxy of luminous suns and gluttonous black holes; what is real and what seems to be real, what is fantasy or seems to be fantasy, cohabit. We are never certain of where we are in *Orlando furioso*, except that we are there.

With Camões it is otherwise. Vasco da Gama's journey is a given, with its shipwrecks, enemy attacks, discoveries and revelations. The marvels it may contain are fantasies only to alien eyes, such as our own at a distance of five centuries. We doubt the existence of mermaids and unicorns, but an early medieval decree gave the Portuguese crown the right to tax anyone who caught a mermaid, and the *Livro das ilhas* refers to an edict from 1461 forbidding private citizens to trade in chilli, civet cats and unicorns.[19] Camões's world is painfully real, in spite of what we might think today of his quarrelling ancient gods and his fantastic bestiaries, and the success of Vasco da Gama's glorious enterprise, predicted in the last canto of the poem by the nymph who tells the explorer of Portugal's golden future, is undoubtedly rooted in the hard-earned experience of a soldier-poet. Even the Island of Love at the end of the quest escapes the brittle realm of allegory: to Vasco da Gama and his exhausted mariners, that marvellous land of Venusian bliss is as real as the feeling of love that must reward every stout-hearted pilgrim.

Is one poem the dark (or light) mirror of the other one? Camões must philosophically reassure us. 'Count nothing impossible', Camões tells his hero (and his readers). 'He who willed always found a way. In the end you too will be listed on fame's scroll of heroes, and this Island of Venus will be yours.'[20] Ariosto, instead, does not require a final moral for his tale. The whole of *Orlando furioso* is its own exultant moral.

17 Luis de Camões, *Os Lusíadas*, Canto V ['Que, por muito e por muito que se afinem / Nestas fábulas vãs, bem sonhadas, / A verdade que eu conto, nua e pura, / Vence toda grandíloca escritura!']
18 Dante, *Inferno* XVI:127–8 ['per le note / di questa comedìa, lettor, ti giuro']

19 Edward Wilson-Lee, *A History of Water: Being an Account of a Murder, an Epic and Two Visions of Global History* (London: William Collins, 2022) p. 39
20 Luis de Camões, *Os Lusíadas*, Canto IX ['Que quem quis, sempre pôde; e numerados / Sereis entre of Heroís esclarecidos / E nesta Ilha de Venus recebidos.']

Two Poems

JOANNA KLINK

The Stone Composures

The whiteness of the headstones
comes to me as warmth. I hesitate
but here I am surrounded by these mute stones,
stunned into a hundred islands whose foglines
reach between weeds. I can hear
the turn of a plow through ground fog
from the neighbouring farm. I can hear a low
beat inside the birch leaves whose branches,
etched black-and-silver, hold back
the humid twilight. If I come
to find they are all gone, I continue on
as a moment of landmass, a switch of breath –
the sheerest souvenir. Standing here,
I am aware of the air filling with unseen
rays. How should I attend
to what I can barely sense.

We shine, unmerited, among the dead we don't
know. My kinship with them now may be
the most of them I know.
Still the stones seem to say you need never
hurry. Though you grieve, you are able to stand
among the carved blocks.

These are the first things: blown trees
in the path of a rainstorm, spotted doves,
the graves in summer.
And the backswept waves you were born into,
the dawn inside frost smoke, foghorns
moving through cells. The evening rains
that seek their shape in you.

Snow, First Night

A thin veiled wash across
the parking lot,

    over heavy asphalt
    sheets. Inside the hospital's
    revolving doors, the grim

hum of machines draws
nutrients and air.
There are beds behind

    every door, a nurse
    pausing between rooms,

a blue tint in the indoor
mist. You might glimpse
a man being erased

    by pain – but it is light that
    sweeps his frame, as sun

might sweep a field. In the long
dusk of the hospital

    chapel backless wood
    benches are laid out for
    contemplation. I'm lost

in myself. The nurses
oblivious to hierarchies
of suffering simply

    attend. Outside the snow
    floats, without colour – lead,

salt, silver leaf – hushing
the highway's bloodroar.

    People in the lot never
    pause – whoever
    enters wants to live.

And above me a red sun
seems to stall in the sky

    behind the snow. How long
    will it stall there.

The snow falls. It falls
against this hour of my life,

    against the ones dying
    inside. It falls
    against the cars

in the lot, that have, for
many nights, not moved.

Six Poems

JEFFREY WAINWRIGHT

Casualty

My manikin model,
for art purposes
articulated
ankle knee and neck,
lies on my desk
half on his back
one arm curiously
stretched into the air
his elbow bent backwards
his featureless face
towards the sky
as though beseeching.

Could a genuine corpse
have this rigidity,
or would its elbow
long ago have
dropped to the ground
alongside the body?
The rigour
holding them,
woodenly at first,
softens
then deliquesces
from the sharp wound
outwards
if not gathered in

Each one like
my manikin
brings to mind
a man of bone and muscle,
limbs once useful

now splayed,
unable to carry
the munitions box,
lips closed
on a tree root
not on his lost canteen.
He is ordinary,
never more than now,
no longer one
who was recognized
by several neighbours
who will mourn him
particularly, resolutely,
as long as
they can bear it,
leaving him at length
to those who sent him here,
the well-dressed,
and well-wrapped,
their as yet unsplintered
regiments like him,
wooden numbers
styled to stand
or run
or wave,
each joint available
until they trip
and fall
torn like paper
arms legs improbable

even in art.

No Philosopher

'I'm no philosopher,' says she
'I like this life too much, I just do',
and she stands outside Tesco
with a trolley-load, piles of tins,
frozen meals, chocolate desserts, dog-food,
Cokes family-size, New Zealand wine.

She wants to cling to what she has
not go seeking other worlds,
abstractions and the like as she once did,
hidden truths always somewhere else,
nowhere near the Tesco carpark that's for sure.

And death always hanging around
forever expecting to be solved
as the soul jumps clear of the body
to live on in its perfect realm
free from the smell of Glade and cabbage.
To think, she says, I was once wrapped up in all that,
trying to look up, always up
and not looking where I put my feet
treading dog-shit into the house.
How did we ever come to think
experience is not real?

She scans the entrance looking for Jay
and his 4x4 coming to collect her and the shop.

She's stranded with not much else to do but think
which she's barely done for years,
not since that finals class with Mike
who showed her what metaphysics could be
to someone who was a shopgirl two years before.

Socrates' mother was a midwife,
but even so she still thinks he was a rum old bugger,
managing to die happy because his soul is free,
the whole world and its storecard points
'dematerialised' into the eternal.
So the remedy for death is death
which doesn't get us very far,
and as for the dream of reason
and the hope of justice both disappointed,
well of course they are,
and now it's coming on to rain,
he'd better get here in a minute.
And this wind as well,
not the wind of thought, oh no,
I should have brought a coat.

She tries to push her trolley undercover
but one of its wheels has just got jammed
and is hard to move.   Is this
what they meant by 'Being?' she wants to know
as the wheel turns sideways
and resists a kick from her newest pumps.
No it's only appearance, the way things
seem to be, inconvenient, noticeable
like birth with its blood and mess
but not important and soon forgotten
for higher thoughts and things.
I liked these pumps now look at them.

She struggles with her phone but Jay's
not picking up.   She'd call an Uber
but you need a password, yes?

Where is Jay?   Did he get the girls from Gym?
He can do his bit now – he stuck it out
in the labour ward, looking for any chance
to feel excluded but always a help.
He picks the girls up, remembers
their Coke and favourite snack,
tries to notice what they are wearing.
He knows that none of us will live forever,
that it's all downhill like when he had to
give up five-a-side last year – there's
Philosophy for you, Man and mutability! –
that procreation is the best that we can do.

Here comes another Ford Fiesta to collect
a woman and her stuff.   Come on Jay
you can't leave me here thinking.

Philippa and Lizzie, both good kids,
polite to their grandparents, do their homework
every night.   What will they make of us?

Will they realise that everything they are,
every thought they take has its origin
in the chance of me and Jay getting together?
That's what it follows from, like me,
in the meeting of mum and dad
one night by the sound-desk they said,
and so on backwards,
back and back and back?

'Poor Reason' amid that much chance,
'a child angered by tiredness that will not sleep.'
I can see that alright.
Our Lizzie was a terrible sleeper
but now she's top in Maths.
'Reason seeks an ending' but also loves endlessness,
wants to close things up, or down,
but then says an argument can have no ending.
That's Lizzie all over, arguing the toss,
never giving in.   Jay says she takes after me.
God help her teachers, she must be a nightmare
to have in class.   What would – or will
she make of Hegel and the causality of history,
eliminating free will.   She'll not have that –
'the unfreedom of the human mind' and
'the compulsions of nature', not likely,
her and her purple hair, bless her.
She's an understander. But suppose it can't be done,
that we must live with the impossibility of truth,
does that mean we cannot be at home
in the world, never could have been?
So what's her Dad up to?

He's a good half hour late now.
How would it be if we had no concept of time?
If we had no concept of change, nor past
present and future and that all we had had to do
was keep things the way they've always been.
I made a note about this and
Australian Aborigines
but Jay's nothing like them
unless he's changed a lot this morning.

It's belting down now and getting cold as well.
Why do we care about that so much?
It's only material after all.
A daft question.
The truth is that's the way we are,
ontologically speaking.   We'll not get past it.
Phil and Lizzie can do a salto
on the vault but only defy the earth
for a moment.   They can't stay aloft
no matter how good their spring
and the landing has to be just right.
No transcendence in gymnastics
whatever it looks like!
Even if they learn the Yuschenko
they won't be able to do it forever
but will stumble into death
probably not getting the landing right.

Enough of that, I've forgotten the hand-wipes again
I'm not going back now.   Jay doesn't use them anyway.
I forgot them.   Am I responsible?

I stopped worrying about the Good Life years ago.
My dissertation on it was good
but what did that amount to?
Is this the Good Life, being able to fill
this trolley, buy the girls new leotards,
have it off with Jay once or twice a week.
That's *eudaimonia* for you!
But there has to be more to it than that.
We've taken on these girls and they must live
virtuously. They'll not learn that by reasoning,
or by looking after #1,
they'll learn by acts, what we do and what
they learn to do.   What I thought about
and wrote about is still busy round the back.

I could do wrong, there's plenty of chance at work.
So sometime could the girls,
and Jay though he'd sleepwalk into it.
But he'd be ready to take the rap,
not think that since the universe is silent
he could get away with it, no one
and nothing to notice and judge
what he has done, or left undone
what he ought to have done.
I made him give up church when he met me
so he probably won't think about it
this way, but he knows he should live
as though there's judgement waiting.
But what's judgement, what's virtue?
The trouble starts with the nouns.

What do I think?   Even Plato and
Aristotle believed we could get it right
eventually, that we could perfect Reason
at least enough to make sense of life, understand
how we can live here as we would want.
But there are others, literary types mostly,
who think it will always be chaos, that the world
will never be amenable to our reason
and to what we can do, what we are capable of.
It's not a world to be good in.
That's why I gave up thinking.
I'd rather be painting the kitchen.

Ah here he is at last
Philly in the front seat for once
and both of them waving like mad.
They must have something to tell me.

Screams in the Night

In this small world
a bird cries in the night,
waylaid by some creature
sharper of eye and claw.

Do we have to think
this is the way of all things,
perhaps even us and our confreres,
must we know it so?

Screams in the night,
must they be lived with?
A new child begins its uttering,
already discomfited.

Comfortable Words

from the Book of Common Prayer

The venerable greybeards of long ago,
'God's conduits',
a hip or a knee gone, toothache everyday,
but still empanelled as wordsmiths
to find the English for the Latin,
the Greek, even the Hebrew
of sandy parchments and –
some of them – to write the litanies,
collects and daily prayers
for those who could abide them,
they knew the truth of things beyond toothache,
felt this *troublesome world*
where we must live, here among
the sins of the world, our *trespasses*,
this *time of tribulation* that is our life,
undone the things we ought to have done,
a reluctant marksman taking aim.

All of this the old men knew
as their eyesight failed,
as they slurped and spilt their soup,

as they tried to *make speed to save us,*
to *refresh* us,
as best they can
with *comfortable words,*

with words anyway
among this trouble:

the normalcy of poverty, hunger,

our better technics,
gunpowder improved

the astute artillerist,
massacres moderated

the nuisance child battered
without mercy

no health in us

Existence

It is not large, but is it large enough,
the world that is,
large enough to be going on with?

No one can assess how much
of everything else there is,
in the universe
as we call it, the *one* thing
much of it without light
or any kind of wind
as far as we know.

But does that matter?
We don't know everything about dolphins
or egrets, or crabs in creeks far away
even though there are some
who work at it
finding new things just to know
what exists,
that there is existence,
as we call it.

Quaker Pegg

An artist who gave it all up.
William 'Quaker' Pegg (1775–1851)

He could not have thought he was no good,
his thistle dish is wondrous,
its spiky leaves, some bent in shadow,
the round purple flower with its dark heart,
all made from his careful studying
of the humble nettle
thriving on Derby's common wastes,
and here translated to a modest plate.

How God is dishonoured in thee o Derby, wrote George
Foxe having had a hard time of it preaching and talking
to the town. Nonetheless more than two hundred years
later William Pegg walked there, a poor man travelling,
and in due time he joined the Friends' Meeting in Derby
a man worthy of communion with them it was said.

Now about the Society of Friends. Foxe the founder told
the Derby magistrate *to tremble at the Word of God.* The
magistrate, unmoved, scoffed *Would you see us quake?*
and ever after the Friends were known as 'Quakers', and
Pegg walked to Derby quaking as he went.

Out of the fire on Horeb,
to Moses, who stood under the mountain,
came the Lord's voice, and only the voice,
nothing seen, no shape, no form,
only the virtue of the voice,
only the purity of the Word,
untrammelled, without a net or hobble
of any kind, out of the midst of the fire,
the Word a simple flame,
nothing to be seen and so graven,
no manner of similitude,
Make no graven image.

And so the Word was felt, not even read,
felt in the breast of the humblest
he and she, felt there as a surety
with nothing else needed, no steeplehouse,
no intercessor dressed to kill,
only the Bible on the table there.
And by this modesty shall you know the Quakers,
guarded in conduct, no ostentation
in colour or in clothes, humble friendship
only to speak as moved. *Make no graven image.*

And from this democracy
came distaste for kingship, lordliness
war and slavery of every kind,
everything that could be called spectacle.

And Pegg looked at his art,
the painting on China plates,
into the sketchbook that he kept,
and he searched his soul diligently
and he saw corruption:

a likeness of a caterpillar along a stem,
a likeness of a beetle, its carapace polished black
        creeping along the ground,
a likeness of convolvulus, its energetic green,
        its blue and white flowers profuse,
a likeness of a moth above a tulip, the flower
        raffish purple, its stamens pressing forth,
a likeness of himself, whiskered, watching.
And he saw corruption.

And he was troubled that the covenant
he had made with his God was forgotten
and that he would not cross Jordan home.

And he gave it all up,
dropped his brush and pen
his sketchbook put away.

The one talent he knew he had
he must refuse at God's express command –
look, there is the Word, do not be led astray.

So he gave it all up, William Pegg,
took back the time stolen from charity,
instead performed selflessly,
gave to whoever had need of his thought and hand.

So, dear reader, what do you think I am up to here?
Should this poem be seen like the thistle dish,
the polished beetle or the convolvulus?
Could the time employed on this or anything else of its sort
be better used in giving aid to refugees,
victims of torture, the cold and hungry
so that they may not be always with us?
The luxury of time, might it not be better spent?
Could I walk with William Pegg,
and follow his renunciations?

Or, might I be permitted to imagine this:
to see you William Pegg in your retirements,
your shawl about your shoulders, your hat pulled down,
stopped on the bridge over the brown stream
to study a lily at the water's edge,
and for one moment release your lascivious eye
to recognize a common thing
that could be attended to?
I am bound to say I hope so William Pegg,
I hope so.

Material for this poem is drawn from *Quaker Pegg* by
George Drury, 2011.

Three Poems

NICKY KIPPAX

Salad days

We were lucky with the weather on the day you died. Unusually warm for the time of year so the perspiration between my cheek and the screen of my iphone surprised me when I couldn't recall your street name for the ambulance: 'For god's sake, it's October!' – I laughed with the operator. The heating was on full whack, not that you'd have been able to feel it, but I remember worrying that the paramedics must be sweltering in all that gear they wear so I hunted for ice in your freezer. Behind the potato waffles was a frost-burned tray holding a single lonely cube. Still, I popped it out and offered drinks before they carried you downstairs. Those spiral steps must've been awkward and I thought I might shout out, involuntarily, like the time you shouted after me when I rode a camel down the motorway with that sweet boy in Sharm El Sheikh. I saw your slippers and cigarettes by the back door and caught myself wondering if you'd need them. Silly. In the police car on the way home I talked about how long those road works were taking at Scarcroft intersection. There was a woman waiting to cross at the temporary lights and honest to god, she was wearing a woolly hat. Slate-grey with a lilac pom-pom. She must've been roasting. I watched her, bewildered, until we'd driven all the way around the bend. When I got home I unpacked fridge things from my shopper and put the kettle on before I told the children you'd died. The oldest, well he just cried and cried and that's him all over but the youngest asked what was for dinner. I thought we could have salad, I remember saying, if it hasn't gone limp in all this bloody heat.

everything must go

sometimes in a department store
we plunder it of buffed mirrors
while escalators jag

we dream away the whole place
we drain it of ambient light
like rude machines

hosiery turns to topiary
spouts hot air and dander

or butterface women
when the polymer's gone

sometimes we go further
mauve and lemon paper
hacking at sequins

peeling back
smelting hi-shine chrome
for christmas – chiffon for spring

crushing on all the blue velvet
using jointed arms

we'll dismantle mannequins
to waft dummy heat

sometimes we unlatch entirely
finding farmers turning scythes

cross over to fields of rye or einkorn
on belted greens – sifting skies

for the scent of rain

Some things shouldn't be so easy

After Kay Ryan

After she dies
I ignore her,
staring at me
from mirrors,
moons, eyes
of my animals.
I blank photos,
avoid her scent,
tracks she wore
into carpets
room to room,
place to place.

So they frame her
speak from
her mouth
show me a body

dressed in best
yellow dungarees
with hands folding
just like hers –
but it's never
really her.

They all say
how sad it is –
so fast, so young –
while I roam our
damn city as if
no-one's ever left it.
Some things
shouldn't be
so easy.

Ğazayı (Khan Ğazı II Giray)

DONALD RAYFIELD

ALEHIERE SVLTAN RE DI TARTARI

Of the forty or so Giray dynasty Khans who ruled the Crimea from the 1440s to the 1780s, at least a dozen acquired a reputation as poets, to match their fearsome fame as warriors. The Crimean Khanate was not just a community of slave traders and 'devils on horseback' whose deadly arrows led the Ottoman army into battle: it was for long periods a prosperous constitutional monarchy, admired for its courts, its religious tolerance, its literacy and culture.

Much of that culture has been obliterated. The Russian invasions of the 1730s burnt down archives, libraries, medreses. A decree by Tsar Nicolas in 1833 ordered 'in the interest of the law' the destruction of any document written in Crimean Tatar language. Very little has survived of nearly 400 years of Crimean written heritage in Chaghatai, Crimean and Karaim Tatar, Ottoman Turkish, Mongolian or Farsi: the printing press came very late to the Ottoman world, and (whatever Bulgakov said) manuscripts do burn. What has survived includes the civil and criminal court registers for a century or two, and poetry that was copied in manuscript anthologies by exiles and by Turks in Anatolia and Thrace.

Khan Ğazı II Giray (1554–1607) was exceptional: his fame as a warrior and musician, as well as poet, meant that his work circulated in Istanbul and has been better preserved than any other Khan's. He was a son of Devlet I Giray, the Khan who burnt down Moscow in 1571 and humiliated Ivan the Terrible (a feat never forgotten by the Ottomans and never forgiven by the Russians). Like most Khans' sons, as a boy he was handed to foster parents in Circassia who returned him in adolescence as a consummate horseman and archer. He was then sent to the Enderun Academy in the Sultan's palace, an institution founded in the fifteenth century and resembling a modern Parisian *École normale*, where promising youths from all backgrounds received a wide-ranging education. At the age of twenty-one he was already in the Crimean army, fighting Moldavians and Cossacks. In 1581, Ğazı was sent by his brother Mehmed II Giray, the new Khan, to fight the Iranians in the almost perpetual Turkish–Iranian war. Ğazı was unhorsed and held prisoner by Shah Abbas in the impregnable fortress of Alamut, where 'high-value' captives were incarcerated. During four years in Alamut in the company of Iranian nobility, Ğazı acquired a perfect knowledge of Farsi, the ability to play and compose memorable chamber music and songs (many still played today), and a remarkable knowledge of Turkish and Farsi poetry.

His first known work was a quatrain in Farsi, a parting message to Shah Abbas, who released him and offered him a bride and a senior army post, both of which Ğazı refused, before escaping back to Ottoman lines, disguised as a dervish:

> There was grief, there was joy, and deprivation:
> Whole ages passed in dreariness.
> What we understood was that in your kingdom
> Any relief is found in forts or dungeons.

In 1588, Ğazı became Khan, on the insistence of the Ottoman Sultan, after the deaths of only two of his four older brothers. Ğazı's radicalism was revealed by his appointment of his older sister as chief diplomat, the Russian Tsar being informed that she was 'in charge of every matter' (Ğazı's senior wife, too, was listed by the Russians as a diplomat requiring payment of a salary). Despite diplomacy, in 1591 Ğazı attacked Russia, to deter it from expanding into Circassia, and was badly wounded.

Russian hostility then abated, and a peace treaty was signed. Ğazı focused on supporting Ottoman campaigns against Poland and Austria. The Turks were losing to Habsburg forces. Ğazı, now known as *Bora*, the blizzard from the north, brought 80,000 men. The Khan was by now known for his love poetry:

> My soul, come as a wall of love this night.
> Let secret wells of love be our candle.
> Whoever looks at you askance, my love,
> May their days be short, their body turn black.
> Drink no wine while my tambour is silent,
> Let a vessel of wine be a vessel of delight.

Now, in 1595, however, he composed for his army his best-known poem, *The Flag*, a typically Crimean Tatar 'Make war, not love!' invocation:

> We don't revere our straight-backed sweetheart, we
>   revere the flag instead;
> Our hearts tangle not in her fragrant tresses, but in
>   banners instead.
>
> Instead of the arrow-like wink of your eyes or brow
> Our hearts are pierced by other arrows instead...
>
> Our favourite pastime is sticking in our sword,
> Instead of enjoying silvery bodies in contact.
>
> Love for a plume on a restive horse's neck

> Has seized us, instead of our beloved's love-locks.
>
> Instead of angel-shaped, gazelle-eyed idols,
> We love a well-schooled, well-paced horse.
>
> We reject alluring houris' moon-shaped cheeks,
> We aspire to martyrdom, glorious jihad, instead.
>
> Our devotion is not to wanton teasing sluts,
> But to hard campaigns, Islamic ideals, instead.
>
> We long with our souls and with God for jihad:
> It's not water we drink, but infidels' blood, instead.

While Sultan Mehmed III valued the Tatar contribution to the war, corrupt viziers constantly undermined the war effort, forbidding the Tatars (who received no pay) to take slaves or loot, and depriving them of rations. Ğazı was as frank in his verse to the Sultan as he had been to the Shah. When the Ottoman-held fortress of Sombor (in north-west Serbia) was besieged by the Habsburgs, he told Mehmed III 'See for yourself... Don't run away from the sword and battle-axe', and wrote:

> If we're embittered, is it any wonder, seeing our
>   patience;
> Sombor's bitter waters, by God, have poured from our
>   noses!
>
> Infidel peoples have ravaged Islamic lands;
> You who fear no God, sit back and just take bribes.
>
> On battlefields we shed our blood, weeping bloody
>   tears,
> While you carouse and pass the wine glass of carefree
>   joy.
>
> If nothing is prepared, our homeland will be lost,
> If you have any doubts, ask the world around you.
>
> O ye wretches, always fighting far from home,
> Now draw the bow of grief with arrows of distress.
>
> The country's laws and state are very ill attuned,
> Ye statesmen, prick up your ears and be alert.

Denouncing the Sultan as 'a contemptible liar, an infidel, the son of a slave girl', and threatening to desert the Ottomans, inevitably, Ğazı was deposed and his younger brother Fetih offered the Khanate. Too late, Sultan Mehmed III realised that this coup would cause uproar in Crimea and in the Tatar army: the Sultan then despatched letters of investiture to both Ğazı and Fetih, assuming that the Crimeans could choose whichever brother they liked, or whichever brother's ship reached Crimea first. The Crimean *mufti*, as supreme religious leader, declared Ğazı to be the legitimate Khan; Fetih retreated to Circassia, intending later to seize the throne. In summer 1597, Ğazı feigned a return to the front in the Balkans, but stopped just outside the Crimean borders: Fetih's coup failed, and he decided to seek reconciliation with his brother. He entered Ğazı's tent near Kaffa, threw off his hat, kneeled and recited lines by the Azeri poet Mehmet Çelebi:

Oh, from the shame you put me to, hurling stones of rejection,
You have gone and sundered my head in two.

As Fetih kissed the hem of Ğazı's gown, a courtier killed Fetih with a blow to the head from an iron mace. (Whether Fetih Giray was anticipating or provoking his manner of death is not known.) Fetih's death was followed by the murder of his nine sons, including an infant at the breast. Ğazı reacted with an improvised couplet:

The heavens have dealt cruelly with Fetih today –
But it is right for mankind on earth and angels in heaven to weep.

In 1598, despite tensions with the Sultan and rumours of his imminent murder by hostile viziers, Ğazı was back in the Balkans. He left the following year, refusing gifts of a fine horse and bejewelled dagger, and then faced an assassination plot in the Crimea, which he forestalled by a massacre of his plotting cousins. In 1602, Ğazı felt it was safe to return to the battlefield. That autumn, as Tatar and Austrian armies stopped fighting and settled down in the town of Pécs for the harsh Balkan winter, an unexpected friendship was born. Ibrahim Peçevi, an ethnic Hungarian, distinguished Ottoman historian and senior official, recalls their friendship:

That winter his Excellency the Khan spent in Pécs. I spent most of the day in his noble company. Sometimes we would go for walks together, or hunting, or on springtime picnics. Sometimes we spent time writing or on other pleasant and laudable activities. He worked on getting your humble servant to learn ta'liq [a Persian pendant script], to prepare the quill properly and he taught me the rules of calligraphy.

Peçevi recalls two long poems by Ğazı, both of which have been lost; one was a dispute between *Coffee and Wine*, a pastiche of the Azeri poet Fuzuli's *Hashish and Wine*. Fuzuli's poem was an allegory in which hashish was personified by Sultan Bayezid, and wine by Shah Ismail; Ğazı's poem may also have had a satirical bent, though it was unlikely to have made a hero of Shah Abbas I. What has survived is Ğazı's 'The Watermill', a pastoral and religious poem, with a surprising flavour of the work of an English country parson of the time:

The Watermill

Travelling, I spied a water-mill. I said.
'Brother, why splash water from your head?

Your chest is flayed, your body bent double,
All round your feet tears form a puddle.

Are you unhappy in love, torn apart?
Pining in exile for the love of your heart?

Have you always complained, by day and by night,
That you had no chance to escape this plight?

What is the reason for such loud lament?
Like an archer's bow, your figure is bent,

You constantly weep, you constantly groan,
Such unexplained grief no human has known.'

The water-mill heard out my well-meaning speech:
A furious response was then unleashed.

'You humans learn by casual chance;
To suffer disaster would alter your stance.

The high mountains used to be my abode,
On me their power and strength were bestowed.

The dry flat wilderness stretched west and east;
When a spring overflowed, it flooded my feet.

All round me my branches reached out like arms;
On the green sward I sang sad psalms.

Francolins clucked, doves cooed in my crown,
And how many flowers sprang up in the ground!

I wore green clothes, in autumn russet, too;
My yellow leaves are now squashed underfoot.

The wind has scattered the violet flowers,
Newly-formed twigs fell down in showers.

On the tulips and the scent they waft
The dew on the ground poured a fatal draught.

At night the daffodils had neither water nor air;
Jujube fruits were men's only fare.

Striking me down, a deadly wind blew:
The film fell from my fading eyes: I knew

My arched body and its dragon's force had shrunk.
Power and strength were drained from my trunk.

They severed my branches, my limbs, struck my bole,
Pierced my feet and bored a large hole.

Next they tied my neck with a rope,
Not a glimmer of joy had I left, nor of hope.

Fields of tulips, flocks of nightingales,
Farewell: I'm overcome by my travails.

They have razed me now down to the ground:
Other than groans I make no sound.

After countless years, my body misbegotten,
My green apparel is black and rotten.

I've been hacked and slashed like Zakariya[1]:
Listen, could any toil be more dire?

I was sawn into planks, they banged nails in my beam,
And, cobbling my timber, plunged me into the stream.

I had to start turning, and I've turned ever since.
You know who did this: it was providence.

My chest is eaten by worms, like Job's,
What cure for my ills can be proposed?

O Khan, do you see the moral of what I'm saying?
You are but a guest in heaven's domain.

Abhor pride, and the world: they are to be feared.
At the sight of the weak, I foolishly sneered.'

Heaven is a monster with seven heads:
It feeds by dispensing humans death.

How many apostles has it served poison to drink,
How many thousands of saints are extinct,

How many Shahs have survived fate's check-mate?
In this game of chess your 'knight' is dead weight.

Here's a wise couplet that a poet proclaimed,
His soul will rejoice if he hears it declaimed:

'Brave warriors look at this world askance,
They waste no time on games of chance.'

Don't be deceived: fate's a treacherous bride,
How many lions, exhausted, have died?

1 As a miracle a tree opened for Zakariya (father of John the
Baptist) to hide in, but a small part of his clothing stuck out.
Satan saw this, took on human form and told the Children of
Israel where Zakariya was hiding. The soldiers then cut down
the tree, killing Zakariya painfully. Qisas al-Anbiyâ, *c.* 1577

False gods, whatever your rank, ignore,
Swear no oath to this world: it is but a whore,

Do not live idly your allotted span,
You still may choose to do what you can.

If perfection is what you strive toward
Then put all your trust in heaven's Lord.

Avoid all care in this world and the next:
Penitent be your tears, compliant your acts.

You've unburdened your heart, Ğazı, now abide!
Act in obedience, let the Law be your guide,

Resign yourself to what fate has wrought,
Know that it's from God, it's from God, from God.

In spring 1683, fighting in the Balkans resumed, and more of Ğazı's cousins were plotting to dethrone him. Ğazı made a separate peace with King Sigismund of Poland and set off home. Sultan Mehmed III had a fatal stroke, and was replaced by the mild and understanding thirteen-year-old Ahmed (who abolished the Ottoman custom of murdering all his brothers on his accession). Ğazı cut himself off from Ottoman control, making peace with the Iranian Shah, and tried to subjugate Circassian tribes instead. As he was returning home in 1607, just across the Sea of Azov he caught plague and died. One of his last poems seems to be an elegy:

At night, unable to sleep, the sad candle sheds tears.
Burning up with suffering, the melting candle turns
  to oil.

Knowing there is no happiness without the beloved,
Like a wounded heart, the candle pours despair.

Expecting a meeting with a friend, the hot candle
  burns.
In the house of peace a lady guest, a secret candle,
  goes out.

From The Coming Thing

MARTINA EVANS

1

JUSTIN said I'd been seen passing a joint on Patrick's Bridge
when I thought I was pure invisible. Escaped. But sure
Knocklong was only twelve miles away. Johnny O'Hare
turned up at a Twenty-First party on Coburg Street –
two thirty-one-year-olds were holding it, ten years late. He said,
Hello Imelda! & I said, *I don't know you,* & turned my back
in my wet-look yellow anorak under the navy sky.
Drowning out home, holding seánces with red-haired Donny &
Dora & Carl near Wilton shopping centre. When Science
became a stranger to me, boiling panic took root.
Cork city & Knocklong merged. When one was above ground,
the other creaked underfoot. Justin's black tar eyes running
everywhere, *'I'll be judge, I'll be jury,' said cunning old Fury.*

2

SOMEONE was singing about not knowing much about
a Science Book. *And what about the French she took?*
Ah she's good at French, Agnes said when I walked in
on herself & Justin roasting mushrooms on the range.
You'd want to keep away from the mushrooms! Justin said
when he saw me. *Have you seen the size of you? Ah no,*
said Agnes. *But remember when she took up Domestic Science*
& dropped the toast in the poached egg water? I remembered
dropping red-hot shortbread fingers, scraping dough off
the cracked blue lino, Justin standing over me. His black
eyes. *Domestic Science, how are you!* Turning the other cheek,
I said, *But I do know that I love you,* & Justin said, *You've*
lost the fecking plot. And I said, *But that's the chorus of the*
song you were singing. What song? said Agnes.

3

JUSTIN said he'd heard I'd dissected a shark with
a handkerchief over my face. Did I think I was
the Ned Kelly of Science? *But Ned Kelly had*
his head in a bucket! Justin said I could write
that down, *I hear you're hanging around with a cheap*
crowd! Old Johnny O'Hare asked in the shop what was
I doing in Cork & Justin said *sweet fuck all* & Old Johnny
O'Hare said, *Oh right so, I'll have Twenty Carrolls & a*
box of red matches. Drove off fast in his powder blue
Cortina. *And he's a fucking wife killer,* said Justin, looking
after him. *You can see his beard growing while he's talking*
to you! Agnes said she said nothing. It hurt her to the
quick *to be even asked.* But someone was giving Justin
information. Like in a police state.

4

DORA'S fierce intellectual, I said. But where did I think
she'd get a job with *Arts*? Justin wanted to know. He
made Arts sound like farts. After I doing Science to be
sensible like Agnes! *She's a bloody female engineer,
can you believe it?* Justin said. I wanted to be unbelievable too.
But it wasn't like school where Sister Joseph's wooden table
was clean, dry, stacked with sheets of pictures of brains &
hearts to be coloured in. Like Holy Pictures, venous blue
& arterial red. Notes on the Reproductive System
handed out silently. No stinking. No dripping. No
dogfish. That desperate army of *Jaws*. Was it even fair
to them? Should they be slaughtered for our education?
I'm thinking about that, too, like, said Dora.

5

DORA said she'd go straight to England if she ever got
in Trouble. She was the youngest of ten & a mistake
& when the priest visited her family, he was bent over,
red with laughing, pointing, *Look at the Mistake!
Hasn't she grown into a fine strong girl!* There wasn't enough
love to go around & only a fool would expect it. Dora was
a Utilitarian. She said there had to be population control.
Like for cats. People couldn't go on reproducing themselves
like they were only brilliant like & they were never objective
about their own blue-eyed boys. *What's the first thing a traveller
will tell a married woman when she sits down in her caravan to have
her fortune told? Your daughter will be successful in catering & your
son will rise to the top of whatever it is!*

6

HOW did some people always know what to do, like?
Dissect a rabbit, cut a plant cross-section for a slide. Poach
eggs & make shortbread. *Silver Spoons & Confidence from Birth,*
said Dora. *Isn't it awful to think there might be no justice?*
I worried along with Dora. Will the first shall be last?
We didn't know. We knew nothing. *Just don't add to the
population in the Name of God!* Dora said & I said I hadn't a
notion of it. I could hardly support *myself* studying
the wrong thing. But Justin wouldn't let me do Arts. I had
to do Science & after that it was supposed to be Computer
Science because that was the coming thing. But really he'd
prefer I did nursing, which was the steadiest job of all.
I'll keep telling you 'til I'm blue in the face!

7

GET a bank loan! said Justin & his face was scarlet not blue.
But I am sure I am on the wrong course! Justin cut me off,
*Anyone who comes along chopping and changing has no character,
no backbone.* His Third Wife Clodagh told me to go easy
on the studying because I was so highly-strung & Agnes
said Arts was bad for the nerves. *Nerves!* shouted Justin.
*No one with Nerves could be that fat. Old Danny Boy has
Real Depression & he's like a pull-through for a rifle.
Coming home with blown-up eyes like an addict after
you've been seen passing a joint on Patrick's Bridge.*
But it was only a rollie washed down with a bottle of Benylin
because of the desperate cough I got when I hit the
blue Gitanes after I left the convent. & that's why I had
to go for the Benylin – for the tickly cough.

JUSTIN thought he was the only man in the world
with a pain or an ache & he was always rolling
up the leg of his trousers to show me the fat blue
branches of his varicose veins snaking around his hairy
red leg. *Look at that!* he said. *And I'm not even fat –*
giving me a disgusted tarry-black look as if I was the
one who should have varicose veins. *How many weeks*
did Seán Mac Stíofáin last on hunger strike? & you can't even get
between breakfast & lunch without a pop? I was sure that
I must be the only girl in Ireland to be subjected to that
kind of leg display by her father. Dora thought she must
be the only child in Ireland to be tormented about being
a mistake by a priest so in a way we were thinking we were
extraordinary too. That's youth for you. It doesn't last long.

Three Poems

MARSHA POMERANTZ

Radius and Ulna, an Aubade with Windows Open

Dear dust, enough said about birds:
squeak boxes feathered in silence,

overheated hearts propelled
branch to branch after nothing.

Nothing gained, then back
again. Their eager airs drift in,

suffusing radius and ulna posed on
radius and ulna, prone on supine,

crossover on parallel, *x* on *ll*. Excuse
this view all anatomic, geometric,

alphabetic, metonymic, dear dust,
x-ray intrusion of clear sight into

the overarching and the under-
stated, this special way of holding

hands. Our still point after eager
osmotic warbles of no bird, when

to and fro flew who? Some me,
some you. Steeple startles the ear,

clanging trochees, ending in *I am*.
Then, dear dust, the mourning dove.

The Expulsion, Again

The Hebrew word for *cunning*, which the snake was from the start, is the word for *naked*, which the folks were by the end. Or what they saw they were, halfway through. His cunning consisted in knowing himself, his nakedness in his own eyes, to say nothing of that tendency to drop his skin. In English *cunning* was first *knowledge*, and only later acquired its tinge of malignity. Here we are, trespassing in the garden, looking to touch likeness, through rain dripping from the points of linden leaves and from the remaining fruit, unspecified but highly coloured.

Why the snake seduced: He wanted company in his nakedness. Tired of being the only one to know how low he could go, even before he was condemned to slither. He was hardly slimy, would enjoy the comfort of a warm, dry hand. We step carefully around uncertainty in Paradise, but despite all caution kick up clods. We notice verbena amid the verdure, hear the bellflower ping, see purple honesty open and close in silence. We spot an orange tube, snake-like, for irrigation, should our compassion run dry.

The kind of tree is unstated in the story so we offspring will avoid the same mistake. But of course it's too late. Ideas dawn as we graze and pluck. Already we sense that sap runs upward in the xylem and downward in the phloem. Some say the leaves called fig came from the tree of temptation, that the Ur-pair used the reveal to conceal. Undress and redress. See how the snail nestles under the nettles. Each creature to its own defense, each defense retaining the tang of danger.

Even as he banished the sinners, the Maker sewed clothes for them from skins: Genesis 3:21. At first we think, what compassion! Then we think: the original *love-by-dice*, *it-hurts-me-to-hit-you*. Were animals slaughtered, or did the snake offer his cast-off selves? By this point our feet are rustling among leaves as our ears detect first frost. Imagine the furrowed brow of God the tailor, the divine mouth full of pins, the tape measure around a neck for the moment gently inclined. Imagine warm, dry hands on nakedness, on the skin over ribs, placing and fitting.

Paid Obits, Thursday's *NYTimes*

Died peacefully throughout her 94 years.
Longtime supporter and distinguished memories.
To carry on his legacy of exceptional sale of Broadway product.
Heartfelt co-conspirator in playful pranks selflessly to the betterment of others.

Bronze Star while serving the guiding force and especially our pianists.
Survived by his adoring kindness and devotion.
Deeply committed to the improvement behind dancer, singer, and loving wife.

Lifelong enthusiast of cherished director making beautiful children's pajamas.
The cause endures but he will be in lieu of flowers.
Friends may call Wednesday sorely missed.
She loved her job.

from *What Is Poetry?*

PHILIP TERRY

'For a poet,' writes Valéry, 'it's never enough to say that *it's raining*. It's necessary... to create rain.' As if in reply to Valéry, Apollinaire's poem 'Il pleut' (1916) descends like wintry sleet down the page from left to right as it threnodises memory and desire, the words descending like rain, becoming rain, which dissipates all in its path. Joan Brossa's pamphlet *Pluja* (1970) takes Valéry's thought even further. Here, there are no words at all. Opening the pamphlet and flicking through its pages, you could be forgiven, at first glance, for thinking the book had been misprinted, as one page after another is completely blank. Until you notice, with a sense of astonishment, that the pages are slightly mottled: each page has been left out in the rain, then allowed to dry before binding. Each page is *written* by the rain.

*

Reading Ted Hughes's 'The Secretary' in *The Hawk in the Rain* – 'If I should touch her she would shriek and weeping / Crawl off to nurse the terrible wound...' – I suddenly realise that the hawk in the rain is Hughes.

*

Any object whatever, e.g. a place, a locality, a stretch of countryside, however beautiful it may be, if it does not arouse some remembrance, is not poetical at all to look at. The same thing, and even a locality or any object whatever which is decidedly unpoetical in itself, will be very poetical when it is remembered. Remembrance is fundamental and of first importance in poetic feeling, for no other reason than that the present, whatever it is like, cannot be poetical; and the poetical, in one way or another, is found always to consist in the distant, in the indefinite, in the vague. (Giacomo Leopardi.)

*

Reading *The Prelude* I am struck by the formality and the poeticisms in the language when Wordsworth is widely thought to have revitalised poetry by shifting it towards common speech.

*

All poetry has a visual element. Even the poems of Philip Larkin depend for their effects on how the words are set out on the page, and sometimes poets – Dylan Thomas and George Herbert to name just two – bring this aspect of their work to the fore, creating visual poems, like 'Vision and Prayer' and 'Easter Wings'. The tradition reaches its apotheosis in the concrete poems of the Brazilian poet Augusto de Campos, and it has had a recent efflorescence in the work of digital poets, such as André Vallias and Eric Zboya. Derek Beaulieu, in *Surface Ten-*

sion (2023), enters this rich tradition armed with Letraset (a largely defunct by-product of the petroleum industry) and digital photocopiers, able to enlarge, reconfigure and distort visual images. The word, in these poems, is all but banished to the margins of the poetic world. If we read the poems closely, we can *find* words – 'rip', 'din', 'lid' – but they concede the arena of the poem, with only a muted cry of protest, to the *letter* itself. It was Mallarmé, in his *Un coup de dés n'abolira jamais le hasard* (*A throw of the dice will never abolish chance*) of 1897 who first unleashed the explosive typographic potential of poetry – here Beaulieu takes this process to its logical conclusion by unleashing the potential of the letter itself. Poem after poem presents a dance of letters, mirroring each other in a palindromic pas de deux, where the eye wanders, unfettered by the pursuit of meaning, into a world of visual display and celebration, as we see arrays of letters shift and turn, distort, enlarge and seek to liberate themselves altogether from the page as they morph in size and shape into ever new forms and potential crystallisations. It's baffling at times, exhilarating too, but Beaulieu throws a rope to the reader – are we 'readers' still as we 'read' this book, or are we something new? – in the form of aphoristic statements punctuating the sequence in place of traditional punctuation, which like words is banished to the margins of this text (only the occasional full stop and comma survives):

These poems begin in recognition: as soon as we see them, we know a particular object is in question because only that object has just this (and no other) emblem.

They aren't stains; they're pools. There's space here, active surfaces, ponds with depth.

Writing is not about something; it is that something itself.

Literature is not craftsmanship but an industrial process where the poem is a prototype rather than artistry.

The contemporary poem is an understanding of juxtaposition. It focuses on the arrangement of letters and material. Headlines, slogans, groups of sounds and letters give rise to forms that could be models for a new poetry just waiting to be taken up for use.

Beaulieu has taken note of the ur-sign of neoliberalism and of capitalism, the ever-present logo, and reinhabited it from the inside, creating logos *without products*, a body of schizoid writing without anything to sell, without an *interpellative* agenda of power and subjection, that frees us from the norms of purchase and exchange. In the book's final sequence, 'Dendrochronology', morphing combines with an accumulative zoom-in, which metamorphoses letters into shapes that bear an uncanny resemblance to the cross-sections of trees: from the origins of Letraset in oil (with all the minings and appropriations of land, and displacements of peoples and habitats that that implies) the poems return us to a state of unfettered nature, to a space that we can once more inhabit, a space where we can play, where we can begin again.

*

I was astounded, reading Michael Schmidt's selection from the poems of George Herbert, in *Poets on Poets*, to read this piece, 'Hope':

> I gave to hope a watch of mine: but he
>   An anchor gave to me.
> Then an old prayer-book I did present:
>   And he an optic sent.
> With that I gave a vial full of tears:
>   But he a few green ears:
> Ah Loiterer! I'll no more, no more I'll bring:
>   I did expect a ring.

What astounds me – it's there in the tone and the music, in the odd choice of words, in the characterisation of Hope, and in the flow created by the generous use of colons (think for a moment what this poem would look like if we substituted dashes) – is the remarkable resemblance to the poems of Emily Dickinson, written some 250 years later. What is one to make of this? We think of poetry – not least the poems of Herbert and Dickinson – as expressions of an *individual* voice, and both Dickinson and Herbert were great innovators of form, of new forms that underpin this feeling that we are in the presence of a distinct voice, coming to us from a specific time and place. But this strange consonance across time would seem to point, with Borges, with Barthes, to the fact that the author has little to do with the work, that the author, rather than expressing themselves in the work, dissolves *into* the work, that it rather belongs to the language, and to tradition, even if, as here, those traditions can lie buried and dormant for centuries, only later to re-emerge in a new flowering.

*

Reading *Paradiso* again, I notice how there are far fewer *ideas* than in the other cantica, how the poem is *less dense*. Is this because the poetry is rising into a transcendent realm, or did Dante run out of gas?

*

Rilke's *Letters to a Young Poet*, written to Franz Xaver Kappus between 1903 and 1908, still have the power to startle. Taken together, the ten short letters, none of them more than a few pages in length, form one of the most remarkable documents on poetry that we have. Near the opening of his first letter, Rilke writes:

You ask if your poems are good poems. You are asking me, but you will surely have asked others before me. You doubtless send your poems out to the magazines and you are distressed each time the editors reject your efforts. You have permitted me to offer you advice, and my advice is that you should give all that up. You are looking outwards and that, above all, is what you should not be doing at this time. There is no-one who can advise or who can aid you: no-one. There is only one way. *You must go inside yourself.* You must seek for whatever it is that obliges you to write. You must discover if its roots reach down to the very depths of your heart. You must confess to yourself whether you would truly die if writing were forbidden you. This above all: ask yourself in the night, in your most silent hour – *Must* I write? If there is an affirmative reply, if you can simply and starkly answer '*I must*' to that grave question, then you will need to construct your life according to that necessity.

This is nothing short of astonishing, for 120 years after the letter was written, it advises the exact opposite of what the industry and academies and schools and mentors would advise a young poet to do in the twenty-first century. It is as if, today, a young poet were advised: forget publication, forget prizes, forget Twitter, forget Instagram, forget networking, forget readings, forget poetry festivals, forget agents – for all of this is 'looking outwards' – look into yourself, then *write*.

*

For Glyn Maxwell, in *On Poetry*, poetry and song are irremediably different. 'Songs are strung upon sounds, poems upon silence... Bob Dylan and John Keats are at different work.' 'It would be nice,' he concludes, 'never to be asked about this again.' But, at the risk of being thrown out of the workshop, I *want* to ask about this again. For one thing, it is not hard to think of examples where poetry and music coalesce, where *poetry* is 'strung upon sounds': Britten's *Les Illuminations* finds its songs in the poetry of Rimbaud, Pierre Boulez's *Le Marteau sans maître* builds its serialist sound world out of the surrealist poetry of René Char. We can think too of songs that are strung upon silence, like any unaccompanied folk song, but this example only makes clear what was staring us in the face all along: all song, all music, is strung upon sounds *and* silence. This is what John Cage reminds us of in his *4'33"*. As so often, it takes an experiment to help us to understand the norm. And in poetry, the very existence of *sound poetry* – as in the work of Bob Cobbing – reminds us that poetry too, like music and song, is strung upon both sound *and* silence. From this perspective, poetry and song have much in common. Why have we forgotten this? In the poetry of John Donne, songs and sonnets sit happily side by side, sound jostling with silence, song with poetry, and perhaps when Eliot wrote of the 'dissociation of sensibility' this was one of the things he had in mind. Sonnet, literally, means 'little song', and many would have been sung to accompaniment on the lute in Donne's day.

Today, though, guitars are for gigs, sonnets for poetry readings. And perhaps this is where Maxwell is coming from. His argument scores high on clarity, but at the risk of oversimplifying our sense of what poetry is, and of what song is, too. For Maxwell song lyrics are not poems, and they don't stand up when written out as poems and removed from their musical underpinnings. This is true of some bad song lyrics, such as David Essex's 'With your love light shining / Every cloud has a silver lining', but it is not true of all song lyrics. Even Bob Dylan, for Maxwell, and he is a big fan, doesn't work as poetry. But is this really so? Here's the opening of 'All Along the Watchtower':

> 'There must be some way out of here'
> Said the joker to the thief
> 'There's too much confusion
> I can't get no relief...'

Dylan deliberately echoes another form of poetry, one that has always remained close to song, the ballad. And like poetry – and unlike David Essex's lyric – Dylan's has the mystery, even difficulty, and therefore resonance, that we typically associate with poetry: who is the 'joker', who is the 'thief', where is 'here'? Like the poetry of Keats, which is full of what Matthew Reynolds has called 'gorielli' – rills, runnels, capillaries – that is, not translations but minute echoes of the words and translations of other writers, such as H.F. Cary's Dante, Dylan too is full of minute echoes of other writings, which include the *Book of Isaiah* ('Prepare the table, watch in the watchtower...') as well as some anonymous Hebrew verse ('How much longer must I wait, like a / look-out on the watch-tower? I am torn / with anguish, I can find no relief'), and Lorca's 'The King of Harlem' ('There must be some way out of here, / some street to flee down...'). For me, this works as poetry, it even demonstrates Eliot's dictum 'Good writers borrow, great writers steal'. And it suggests that Bob Dylan and John Keats might not be at such different work after all.

*

Reading *Martial in English* it is startling to encounter the poems of Ben Jonson again, and to realise for the first time that the best of them – 'On My First Sonne', 'Inviting a Friend to Supper', and 'To Penshurst' – are not *original* poems, but *versions* of Martial.

*

Nightingales and poetry. The poetry of nightingales has a long and rich history, stretching from Persian and medieval literature to the Renaissance and Romanticism. Among late nineteenth-century poets, John Clare is unusual in treating nightingales as part of natural history – in Clare's poems, minutely observed, a nightingale is a nightingale, and we can learn from his poems that nightingales use 'dead oaken leaves', 'little scraps of grass' and moss in constructing and lining their nests. More commonly the bird takes on a mythical dimension, either, as in Keats, as a bird whose rich song transports us to another world, far from everyday cares, or else in the pastoral tradition. There, the mention of Philomel at once fulfils the pastoral expectation of an idealised beauty, before cutting through that idealisation to disclose the dark side of the landscape: in the ancient myth related in Ovid's *Metamorphoses*, the bird stands in for sexual violence. Philomel, in Ovid, is raped by her sister's husband, Tereus, and to prevent her from telling anyone he cuts out her tongue and imprisons her. Yet she tells her story, indirectly leaking it to her sister Procne by making a tapestry which depicts the scene of rape. Once Procne learns what has happened she plots a terrible revenge in which Tereus is fed a meal consisting of his children, before, in the final scene of pursuit, Tereus is transformed into a Hoopoe, Procne into a swallow, and Philomel into a nightingale. When Keats refers to the nightingale's 'full throated ease', he too seems to be making an oblique reference to the myth, for while it is true that the nightingale sings with its throat – one of the things that makes its song distinctive, giving it the power of a motor at full-throttle – the myth explains *why* the nightingale sings with its throat rather than its tongue: it has no other option. In this point the myth predicts what was later confirmed by natural history, though in nature it is the male bird that sings rather than the female, to attract a mate in the first instance, and to protect its territory in the second. The nightingale and the poet, then, have at least two things in common, both of which help to explain the bird's ubiquity in poetry: they are both supreme songsters ('full-throated ease' could well be applied to the poetry of Keats as well as the song of the bird), and they are both densely coded, metaphoric (the nightingale is rarely just a nightingale). A third thing they have in common is *indirection*: Philomel cannot express herself directly, so has to express herself *by means of* a tapestry; and poetry is also an art of indirection: Dante cannot climb straight up the mount of Purgatory to reach Paradise, as he tries unsuccessfully to do at the start of the *Inferno*; instead he must first descend into the spiralling circuits of Hell. And as soon as I say this I see a fourth thing they have in common, and a fifth, perhaps more. The nightingale is a migrant, like Philomel, who is forced to leave her homeland in Greece to move to Thrace, and in this the bird is like Dante, banished from Florence, as well as any poet – Celan, Brodsky, Mandelstam – who is forced to live in exile. Then there is the tongue, or rather its removal, depriving Philomel of speech. Unlike Philomel, no poets I can think of have literally had their tongues removed – Orpheus, even after he is dismembered by the maenads, still has his tongue and carries on singing – but metaphorically they often find themselves voiceless, sometimes through censorship, sometimes through the simple inability to articulate what they wish to say in everyday speech, or in their mother tongue. So T.S. Eliot starts imitating French poetry, or *writes* in French, learns Greek, German, Sanskrit, studies the classics, or amasses strings of quotations. The greatest poetry, in a word, is often written in the search for a voice, in order to say what could not otherwise have been said, because the poet has no voice that can easily express what they wish to say, no tongue with which to speak their innermost thoughts. Recently, I was forcibly reminded of this in what was for me a rare, if not unique, epiphany. I was in the caves of *Les Colombelles* near the village of Les Eyzies in France, researching Paleolithic art for *The Lascaux Notebooks* (another work of indirection, ascribed as it is to the invented poet, Jean-Luc Champerret), when a drop of water fell on my head. The guide laughed, and said that that drop of water, from the moment it fell as rain, would have taken fifty years to work its way through the limestone layers above the cave before it fell on my unsuspecting head. And then I realised that the raindrop must have fallen in my childhood, when I was living in Belfast, and still spoke with a Belfast accent, long before I moved to England, and had that accent forced out of me by jaunts and bullying at school. And as I realised this, I realised too that my long search for a way in which to write, which had now taken me deep into the earth, perhaps had its origin in this extinction of my voice round about the age of thirteen. It was later the same day that I had a revelation that was key to unlocking the poetry that went on to form *The Lascaux Notebooks* – I suddenly realised that the three-by-three grids that were to be found in Lascaux could be filled with signs found in the cave, and that these grids, once filled with signs, might then be deciphered to make poetry.

*

Bad Poetry. Reading *Hidden Poems* by Jordan Davis, a fantastic and endlessly inventive collection, I'm immediately won over by the opener, 'Bad Poem', which consists of a single line: 'Put that rock down'. I like it, but am hard-pressed to say why. Is the poem, or poet, caught in the act of 'being bad', that is, about to throw a rock? Is it therefore a plea *not* to be 'bad', to put down the rock and do something less aggressive, such as write poetry, even bad poetry? And in that it makes me think, is it really a 'bad poem'? It doesn't rhyme, it's too short, without being epigrammatic, it won't be considered for any prizes, it might even be a bit silly, so not 'serious poetry'... though it *is* enigmatic, sometimes seen as the hallmark of 'good poetry'. And it makes me think too about the importance of bad poetry. Not necessarily the kind of bad poetry we find in collections that more or less announce themselves as such, like *Worse Verse*, published by the *Sunday Times*, which tend to be collections of doggerel, indirectly giving vent to a fundamental dislike of all serious poetry, but poetry which is irregular, jarringly rhymed if at all, even clunky in its flow, rough rather than smooth, like the poems of Juvenal when compared to Horace, say, plain, straightforward. Not all poetry needs to be like Keats, or Mallarmé. We need the rough along with the smooth, the cracked along with the polished. Each time I finish a new collection, the last thing I do is to roughen it up a little, just as an artist might rub sandpaper over a canvas, or spill wine over it, or even throw some rocks at it. Broken, limping, carrying stains, dents, the poetry can reveal its human side, is ready to step out into the world.

Bibliography

Apollinaire, Guillaume, *Selected Poems*, transl. Oliver Bernard (London: Penguin, 1965).

Beaulieu, Derek, *Surface Tension* (Toronto: Coach House Books, 2022).

Brossa, Joan, *Poetry Brossa* (Barcelona: Macba, 2017).

Champerret, Jean-Luc, *The Lascaux Notebooks*, ed. Philip Terry (Manchester: Carcanet, 2022).

Carmi, T. (ed.), *The Penguin Book of Hebrew Verse* (London: Penguin, 1981).

Dante, *Paradiso*, transl. Robin Kirkpatrick (London: Penguin, 2007).

Davis, Jordan, *Hidden Poems* (Durham: If a Leaf Falls Press, 2022).

Hall, Allan (ed.), *Worse Verse* (Manchester: The Philips Parks Press, 1971).

Hughes, Ted, *The Hawk in the Rain* (London: Faber, 1957).

Leopardi, Giacomo, *The Canti* (with a selection of his prose), transl. J.G. Nichols (Manchester: Carcanet, 1998).

Lorca, Federico García, *Selected Poems*, ed. Christopher Maurer (London: Penguin, 1997).

Reynolds, Matthew, 'The gorielli – rills – capillaries of translation' (lecture delivered at the Italian Cultural Institute, 21 October 2014).

Rilke, Rainer Maria, *Sonnets to Orpheus* with *Letters to a Young Poet,* transl. Stephen Cohn (Manchester: Carcanet, 2000).

Schmidt, Michael, and Rennison, Nick (eds.) *Poets on Poets* (Manchester: Carcanet, 1997).

Sullivan, J.P., and Boyle, A.J. (eds.) *Martial in English* (London: Penguin, 1996).

Valéry, Paul, *Poèmes et Petits poèmes abstraits, Poésie, Ego scriptor,* ed. Judith Robinson-Valéry (Paris: Gallimard, 1992).

Wordsworth, William, *The Prelude: The Four Texts*, ed. Jonathan Wordsworth (London: Penguin, 1995).

Four Poems

CATHERINE-ESTHER COWIE

Mimorian

after Carlos Drummond's 'Resíduo'

Only a little of me remains, a fixture,
Madwoman locked in a downstairs room,
four-walled gag, muffler. Of my ravings,
the upstairs hear nothing, nothing.
But still a little of me will stay, the stink of me
in the sheets, on the walls, on their tongues,
wagging, wagging all night long about
my bad romances – chupid woman,
sad woman
        object lesson.

Of my illness, they talk too much,
I am spectacle, spectre, fire-lover
wandering off into the bush, the market square.
My early morning peep shows, the breaking
day, someone forgot to lock my room, again,
the music loud in my head, how I shook,
shook the neighbourhood awake with my naked breasts,
my grandchildren cried, their friends can't come over.
And of those things I remember
so little
      so little
why can't they *do* the same?

Of the things I enjoy,
they won't remember, the mourning doves
nesting in the monstrous breadfruit tree,
rum thrown back, going deep
down, deep down between my legs,
my hair brushed and slick and smoothed
into a bun, my yellow satin ribbon.

Of God, am I against, for
or indifferent, they've never asked
or cared to know. My mother,
father, their names...
already they've forgotten.
Of my love of white, they'll remember
cotton dresses bleached in a blinding sun,
my men, always, always fair.

Of me so little will remain, stripped
and pared down to a fear,
bright and blossoming in the back
of a young girl's head: ou fou ou fou
ou fou
        ou fou.

The Outside Child

I will not disappear,
dead myself in a bush somewhere.
The freak lives, sucks air.
I have a face that is not so unlike hers.
Perhaps that's what troubles,
I am the final blow. The betrayal,
so close, under her roof, in her bed.
The man she so loved, loved me,
raised me in her house, unnatural thing that I am,
a sin, offspring of a predator and a prey,
that grows and grows, has a mammalian face,
hands, feet, a voice like the blackbirds,
high-pitched and singing.

I have the wildest dreams, to hug her children –
my cousins. My brothers and sisters.
Daughter of a sketel, mother-killer, they insult,
I blossom bright, draw nearer still, allow their biting,
bites. The sharp of their teeth, the only intimacy
they will give, the taste of my flesh, an epiphany,
      I am, love me.

Daughter

Curious thing. Spit and flesh.
Huge black eyes.
You weren't ugly. That helped.
And wasn't I tender?
Gathering you to my warmth,
your lolling head, breakable body.

And of the hate I brewed and brewed
while you were tethered inside,
you bore no mark of it,
no trace of your forced conception.
You came out well-formed and wailing,
and I felt nothing.
But knew you were mine.
Mineness. A feeling. Is there such a thing?
Like owning a cat. A thing to do.
A small butt to wipe. But wasn't I tender?
Isn't that why you beg me not to leave, my tender looks.

Listen: I fed you, so that I could be fed.

Haven't I lived like a prisoner,
my survival threading through your squalling body?
But now you are weaned and walking,
a body not so flimsy, so tender.

And I am but twenty-two, full of shadows
and shadowing,
there are things my teeth edge for.

Already I have gone, out of mind
into that crooked picture on the wall, there.
What am I but that long road running
through those watercolour fields.

If you follow, I warn you,
I will be as much a weight around your neck
as you have been around mine.

Rescue

The freak, dark-haired beast knocks
at my cupboard door.
I have kept quiet, not a sound,
even when the daddy-long-legs
mounted my nose.
She has sniffed me out,
calls, *Mommy.*

What terrifies, the oven, the flour,
the butter pooling on the counter.
What a test of love,
my husband wants homemade bread,
It's easy, he said.
What a test of love,
to understand the workings of a clock,
a rug,
a water filter,
the proportion of yeast
to flour,
the measure of a dash,
a dab,
a dabble of salt,
a Ms. Fixer-upper,
Maker-of-things
I am not.

The bread is hard,
hard like a rock,
it will break the teeth
of our guests coming for dinner.
O what terrifies,
he'll turn into Mama,
how you kah cook up to now?

My daughter knocks again.
She is four, a voice so sharp, a seam-ripper.
I lead her to the sea roiling
at the back of our house,
our arms full of bread rolls, stones.
What is a daughter,
small rescue tearing
towards the shoreline,
rolls falling like a trail of droppings.
She flings the bread into the waves.
I will tie my waist with a string to hers,
                    my little buoy.

Three Poems

GER DUFFY

Coffee with Peter

Peter arrived in a taxi, we were just in time
to see the Jack Yeats, all those blues made me
feel sad. On the way, in Stephen's Green
a man and a woman balanced on a rope strung
between trees, she kept falling. After a while,
I stopped looking. Tall yellow trees wrestled
their skirts at us and swore. Cyclists flitted past
dropping packs to junkies in shrubs. Peter said
he knew a rooftop café we should try, I wanted
to go to the Shelbourne but they were only serving
residents, we decided not to go to MoLi after all.
Overhead a loft of pigeons swooped figures of 8,
my feet began to hurt. The café was indoors so
I didn't consider it rooftop, the girl there didn't
know what a small americano was. Buskers sang
'*You'll never walk and alone*' in Grafton Street. Dave
told Peter of his diagnosis. Peter stopped talking
about his poetry, we watched crowds of shoppers
laden with bags and flowers. People stood in pub
doorways to see Liverpool go 5–0 against Man U,
Dave said Devine*, the 97th, had died in July.
A junkie sat still as statuary, as if he had been
dropped from the sky, his grey shirt flapped in
the breeze. We swayed down Grafton Street,
cold teasing our teeth, holding on to each other
as streetlights turned our faces grey and all we might
have said was silenced by the scream of sirens.

* *Paul Devine was the 97th victim to die from the Hillsborough disaster.*

Dublin Temperance Society Visitation Report July 1911*

A dreadfully licentious man living with two daughters,
Florence and Mabel in a basement hovel at 20 Gardiner Street.
A widower, he sleeps in the hardbacked chair, both girls
share a mattress. I could hear him singing, *The Last Rose
of Summer* from the corner. Prior to this address they stayed
at Hishons Hotel *where he feared for his girls' morals;*
prior to that they were evicted from a dwelling in Fontenoy
Street. Mewling like a kitten, the youngest has been ailing
for the past week, newly deaf, feverish – typhoid, I fear.
I would pay doctor's fees but his landlord, Mr Sloan,
assures me his tenant has a good pension from the Customs
House, which is spent in Kennedy's pub. When I warned
him of the demon drink, he kissed both my hands, cried
that I reminded him of his dead mother. He is well spoken,
wears a suit, but I fear the whole situation is beyond any
redemption, his name is Joyce, a Mr John Stanislaus Joyce.

* *Mabel Joyce (younger sister of James) died of typhoid, in July 1911.*

Ubatsute*

On my first visit, he was taken to a locked
bathroom where I heard him cry, then beg
them to stop and because I was asked
and they were now in charge, I waited outside.

When the Sister phoned to say there had been an incident
I was not surprised, because although nothing
he said was logical, he told me that he was left naked
for hours and that the aides were all bla'guards.

The incident involved an aide placing
a plastic bag over my father's head,
every time he spoke or tried to speak.
My father, the Atlas of my childhood.

The Sister said the management were sorry,
they were doing their best, meaning
they would keep him there in his wheelchair
a stalagmite in front of daytime TV.

He was moved between bed, chair and toilet,
politely asking nurses to direct him to the road
home, meaning his childhood home.
Father, this is your mountain, beware the wolves.

*An old Japanese myth where offspring carried their aged parents on
their backs in times of famine, to abandon them on the mountain.*

Saint Robert of Waco

RORY WATERMAN

'I'm a wacko' from Waco, ain't no doubt about it.
Shot a man there in the head but can't talk much
    about it.
He was trying to shoot me, but he took too long to aim.
Anybody in my place woulda done the same.
I don't start fights, I finish fights, that's the way I'll
    always be.
I'm wacko from Waco, you best not mess with me.

That's not me embracing a new poetic direction, nor is it about gun-hoarding and -slinging cult leader David Koresh and the Branch Davidians, names synonymous with Waco worldwide since the Waco Siege in 1993. Rather, it is the opening verse to a hyper-masculine, apparently autobiographical barnstormer by the late Texan country singer Billy Joe Shaver, recalling an 'incident' in 2007, when an argument broke out in a bar after another man flirted with his wife. (Shaver, who claimed to have shot the would-be lothario 'right between the mother and the fucker' – face tattoos, perhaps – was acquitted.) In any case, in September last year I spent a couple of weeks in central Texas, with this song lodged in my head thanks to a friend who had sent it to me via WhatsApp on my first day in town.

My happy duty in Waco, before I was to have some time to myself out in the wild Texas Hill Country to the west, was to spend a few days at Baylor, the world's biggest Baptist University, to give a reading and a workshop, and attend a class for students who had been set my third collection, *Sweet Nothings*. Professor Kevin Gardner – one of those people we occasionally hear about, who buys and reads poetry but doesn't tend to write it – was my host, and a very affable and entertaining one, too. Kevin is a John Betjeman specialist, which must be a lonely pursuit in Texas. After a friendly classroom interrogation by his students, there were several hours to kill before the reading, which was to take place in the Armstrong Browning Library. We had a big Texan lunch, peered into the Baylor University bear enclosure ('my university's campus has pigeons and wagtails', I told him), and then Kevin presumably tired of my enthusiastic naivete and left me with his equally affable colleague Professor Sarah Ford at the front of the Armstrong Browning Library, so that we might look around. Okay, fine. I'd never heard of it.

Neither have many of the citizens of Waco, I suspect – perhaps even including some of the students at Baylor. They ambled along the bosky paths outside, slurping iced coffees, clutching books and gazing into phones, like extras on an excessively perfected campus-based film set. The Library, pointedly in what locals think is 'Italian Renaissance-style', loomed like the all-American attempt at elsewhere that it is. It was built in the late 1940s, to house what was already at the time the world's largest collection of artefacts related to the lives and writing of Robert and Elizabeth Barrett Browning. How Dr A.J. Armstrong, then chairman of Baylor's English Department (once housed in the same building, before the expanding collection evicted it) acquired the wealth to do this remained mysterious to me throughout my visit, but in 1912, when the Brownings' son Pen died, his possessions were auctioned by Sotheby's in London, and Armstrong raised the final paddle.

We entered the sudden dim, glad to escape the sun, but were then prompted by a sprightly guide ('Hi!' – big outstretched hand – 'I'm Caleb!') to step back out and inspect the huge bronze doors through which we'd come. They are modelled on Ghiberti's famous Gates of Paradise in Florence, though here the ten panels depict scenes from Robert Browning's poems. It is a fitting introduction to what is effectively a cathedral-sized secular shrine. Back inside, we sauntered across the empty entrance hall, our footsteps rebounding from the marble floor, the marble walls, the frescoes depicting more scenes from Browning's poems, and some of this building's many heavy stained glass windows glowing with yet more scenes from Browning's poems. Most of them were obscure to me, and remained so, because Caleb didn't know what they depicted either – and I don't blame him, because they are so bountiful, and so evidently the product of a deep, narrow devotion. Across from the door, a huge painting of Robert, by Pen, stared down like a beneficent saint, over his final writing desk, placed on a dais at the back, as though it were an altar.

Next, we followed Caleb to the Foyer of Mediation, the inner sanctum. A giant chandelier hung tiny from its shallow dome, which glinted away dully in 23 carat gold leaf. An Italian garden scene with Classical adornments covered the upper walls, along with a few quotations from even more of Browning's poems, some tempting awkward comparisons:

Man's work is to labor and leaven –
As best he may – earth here with heaven;
'Tis work for work's sake that he's needing.

We were then pointed towards a little apsidal alcove at the back, the 'Cloister of Clasped Hands', presumably named thus for its alliterative properties. And there, on a little plinth, was Harriet Hosmer's famous bronze sculpture from 1853, made from a plaster cast of the couple's hands gently gripping one another, hers on his, each lopped cleanly at the wrist, homely and unheimlich. 'There are no contemporaneous portraits of the two together', said Caleb. 'This is the closest we've got'. So near and yet so far.

Walking around these grandiose rooms, it is obvious Elizabeth has lost the battle for wall space. 'So Elizabeth has the upper hand, but only literally', I quipped, feeling clever and then wondering whether this gets said at least a couple of times a day. The dynamic changed a little upstairs, in the comparatively cosy Elizabeth Barrett Browning Salon, the five stained glass windows of which depict five of her *Sonnets from the Portuguese*. Her writing chairs, tables, cabinets, were dotted around. A fat silky rope kept us at a polite distance.

'Do you have many, er, books or manuscripts?' I asked. Oh yes, and there are also very quiet reading rooms in which to consult them. The library is proud to have 25,000 visitors a year, but that's fewer than seventy a day. Electrons in an atom, not sardines in a tin. We stopped a moment at a sleepy reading room, the sort one imagines the British Library might have until one has actually been into any of its bustling counterparts, but I hadn't prepared myself for this place, wouldn't have known what to ask for nor why I wanted to see it, and besides, we were running out of time. Some manuscripts are displayed in the hall where I was to read that evening, though most of the ample cabinet space there is given over to a bricolage of first-rate curios: illustrations of the Pied Piper by the ten-year-old boy for whom Robert Browning wrote the poem; the Brownings' carriage clock with 'Bates Huddersfield' engraved on it; and what is Robert's last known bit of versification in his own hand – 'Here I'm gazing, wide awake, / Robert Browning, no mistake!' – beneath a pencil sketch, and dated 'Nov 24 '89', two and a half weeks before he died.

Of course, the Brownings had no idea their personal items and jottings would ever be on display here – nor, surely, that 'here' existed. When Robert died, Waco had only just started to outgrow its role as an outpost for cattle herders on the Chisholm Trail, the Wichita Indians having been forced out of the area a generation earlier. When Elizabeth died, it had comprised only a cluster of wooden buildings. 'Italy / Is one thing, England one', wrote Elizabeth Barrett Browning in 'Aurora Leigh', and that played in my head, but Italy and England have far more in common with one another than either does with Waco, even though the meagre Texan towns of Windsor and Milano and Clifton and Italy (and Eulogy) are each within an hour's drive.

On my final morning in Waco, a poet friend in New York sent me a message: 'Are you going to visit the Siege site before you head out of town?' I'd looked it up, of course, and had briefly considered doing so. A significant proportion of those who died during the Waco Siege had been recruited by the Branch Davidian leadership on a visit to England; several came from Nottingham, where I live; some of their relatives still reside within a mile or two of where I write this later, a few months later.

The victims were exactly that, whatever you make of their religious beliefs: victims, often inherently vulnerable ones, who had in most cases done nothing more malignant than seek a meaningful life, and who ended up instead dying in a manifestation of hell on earth. They deserve to be remembered, but does one ever visit such a place *only* to remember? And what could I gain from going to look at a plot of earth? In any case, I traced my way through the raggedy suburbs of Waco and down country lanes through nondescript prairie, towards where the New Mount Carmel Center complex had been until it burned down and destroyed nearly eighty people in the process, many of them children, some to the extent that their autopsy records read 'sex undetermined'. I am not a believer, but this is sacred ground.

The long driveway up to where the Center once stood is lined with sparkling granite memorials, some donated by Texan militia groups. Perhaps unfairly, I am reminded that white supremacist Timothy McVeigh murdered nearly two hundred people in Oklahoma City, two years to the day after the tragedy here, in supposed revenge at the government. What had happened to the Branch Davidians quickly became not just a rallying cry for those of all political persuasions who questioned perceived governmental overreach, it also became a white supremacist cause, though the Branch Davidians unceremoniously killed in that compound had no such affiliations; in fact, a high proportion of them were black. A simple little clapboard chapel now stands where the building was, a 'TRUMP 2024' flag fluttering above it. Inside, Alexa Pace, the wife of the current pastor of the now greatly diminished Davidians, was very excited by my furtive entrance – I was the only visitor, after all, and she soon discovered I had 'an accent', which is all it usually takes in smalltown America. She pressed a bullet casing from the initial raid into my palm and asked me to take it home. 'Oh, my son used to dig them up all the time.' Snatches of Bible prophecy, eye-watering anti-government propaganda and photographs of those who had burned to death all around us covered the walls like posters in a very odd teenager's bedroom, as David Koresh's music (he'd once dreamed of being a rock star) thumped from a speaker at the volume of shopping mall muzak. Horses cropped grass beyond the open double doors. She guided me past them, past the former swimming pool where turtles appeared and vanished in green water, across the scrubby lawn where the Center's vault had been and where several bodies had been recovered from among the cinders, and into a former storm shelter, now just a weed-strewn concrete pit with butterflies jinking in its stillness. A huge iridescent dragonfly landed on a big bloom I can't name. I opened my palm and looked at the little nub it cradled. It would have been gauche to cry. Why did I come here? Why was I glad to have done so? And more lines from 'Aurora Leigh' came to mind, more or less, although I had to wait until I was back in the car before I could look them up and remember them properly, out of context in every way and perfectly apt for all that:

'And see! is God not with us on the earth?
And shall we put Him down by aught we do?
Who says there's nothing for the poor and vile
Save poverty and wickedness? behold!'
And ankle-deep in English grass I leaped,
And clapped my hands, and called all very fair.

In the beginning when God called all good,
Even then, was evil near us, it is writ.
But we, indeed, who call things good and fair,
The evil is upon us while we speak;
Deliver us from evil, let us pray.

Eight Poems

MILES BURROWS

1. Tea Dancing in Litzi-Ruti

Young men's poems may be forgiven.
For the old, there is really no excuse.
I said – Beryl, we don't want any theatricals.
We stayed at the Grimpenhorn
Close to the skilift.
At *Silvesterabend* Mr Beilick said I should wear a hat.
And Uncle Ed

Did his impersonation of King Farouk.

I went to a Hungarian in Chester Mews
You know how some people hold on,
Practising tango in the kitchen
But it's not the same without a partner.

2. Not Too Late

It's not too late to go on the stage
As a butler in Australia.
I'll refer it to the ethics committee.
When you danced
Men were rising up for you
Like all the cornstalks of Asia.
I went through life with the emotions of a drama critic.
You brushed your teeth like a flautist
Holding the brush in both hands
Negotiating a tricky passage in Hindemith.
Everyone's writing their memoirs
Except you. People I knew
Have all grown shorter over the decades
Like short stories that have been edited.

3. At the Florist's

As a poet, you can get a job in a florist's –
Moyses Stevens
On Hay Hill, if you are in that part of London,
Though parking is difficult. Green Park
On the Piccadilly Line. Little birds' nests
With a couple of wood anemones in moss
Sprinkled with morning dew that glistens
And a real mist. You meet interesting people
And in summer you can pull down a striped awning.
You have your spray and your can. Don't get drawn
Into polishing leaves. Across the roads
There's a coffee shop
So you can mingle with students and artists.
Have a copy of *Züricher Tageblatt*
Which you can't read. This can be helpful
In inducing a trance-like state
Called negative capability.
If you don't know any threatened flowers, refer to
Fisher's chapter – *'Hangers On, Casuals, and Fugitives'.*

4. Horlicks
(An English airman considers his options)

We've got a real Horlicks here.
I'll just give you a heads up then hand you over to Ben.
If you get locked into an event in time and space get
   rid of it.
We can improve definition
Beyond that, we are hitting a brick wall.
It's a question mark.
Unless we take the outside world out of the equation.
I came off like a mad cat. What I will say to you
Is this is a most disorienting platform. Any questions?
Yes?
– Can I play rugby beforehand sir?
– Who's the jockstrap? It's a maturity issue. It's a
   macho thing.
An awareness issue. Don't dwell on anything
Because really we should be perfect.
– Thank you sir.
– Anything else?
– Is it all right to have a drink beforehand, Sir?
– If we're talking Armageddon what's a pint of
   Boddingtons?

5. The Piano

The piano makes a faint noise
Like my aunt's Jack Russell used to make
Listening to the *Pearl Fishers*
Or as a meadow brown folds its wings
To resemble a dead leaf
The desire to speak is a poised vibration
Sigh once in a controlled way.
I'll get it to take a bit of the chaconne
Gently but firmly
Like getting a bit into a horse's mouth
While it's standing on your foot.
A piano always knows when you're nervous.
White moths in the sunless dampers
Skitter blindly in their interrupted dreams

6. A Freshman at the Porter's Gate

Don't be a *dilettante*
Be promising. Presentable.
Self-contained as a drowned cathedral.
Maybe I'll choose philosophy or very ancient history
A few fragments of yesterday's news
In an alphabet no one could read.
Philosophy comes nearest to the Occult.
I'll be a hermit by a waterfall

While hosts of Midian pitch their tents
In diaries of non-events
And Madame Arcati's calling for a *slow curtain.*
My tutor's not eccentric as I hoped,
But sprays on a sample of Estee Lauder
That brings on a pleasing thought-disorder:
I feel like a Grecian urn
Being lowered into the ocean by Jules Verne.

7. Pearl Fishing

What is it about upright pianos
That makes you feel they would rather be lying down?
The tuner says there's some life in it yet
Though... here he is silent and plays a few
Enigmatic bits. Like a car which has done 100,000 miles, this piano
Has done so many rachmaninovs
Been bogged down in so many brahmses, picked itself up after so many bits of bach
And every one of them has left its scar, its pothole.
The piano moths scuttle around when the top is opened
And you look down into a pit. Some notes are silent
As people under interrogation. The harder you hit them
The more obstinate they are. Others, the white ones
Like snowdrifts on the way to Moscow, waiting for armies to give up
Or winter to change.
It could all be so easy if I could hit the right notes.
Or keep an eye on the music.

I have the feeling. For Fauré's *Elegy*
Played by a child on a cello on a summer evening in the next house
Sometimes it hums to itself, like the Jack Russell
My aunt had which would cry out
When she played the *Pearl Fishers.*

8. For Death, Press One

For death, press one.
For all other enquiries, please hold.
Thank you for calling death
You have the option to hold (1) or let go (2)
Thank you for holding. My name is Frannie. Short for Francine.
Please be patient with us at this difficult time.
On a scale of 1 to 5 please grade your difficulty.
If you are calling about a loved one, press 1,
If it is about someone you feel a social obligation towards, press 2.
If it's about someone you wish you had loved but now it's too late, press 4.
You have pressed 11,
11 is not an impatient form of 1. It is its own number.
A *cartouche* is a kind of frame for a hieroglyph,
It is a French word rhyming with *louche* or *barouche.*
I knew a girl at school they said was *farouche.*
I sometimes think of her even now.
Not all the time of course.
It is like looking into a driving mirror.
If you are driving pull in to a designated parking space.
If you have a smart phone and a film of a mourning chaffinch, press one.
Thank you. You have pressed mourning chaffinch.
My name is Francine.

Eight Taiwanese Poems

A collaboration between

EVAN JONES AND SHENGCHI HSU

On collaboration, Evan Jones writes:
The notion of translation is suspect, I know. The tongues of the reader – of the language into which the work is translated – and the bilingual expert roll along as if seeking out inconsistencies. And inconsistency is where a good translator of poetry lives, maintaining the impossible balancing of form, music, meaning. What is least obvious is that form travels a straight line pretty much between languages and cultures. Form is often the easy part of translation. Music requires ability and understanding of tradition as well as the workings of a language. But meaning struggles. How do I translate something like 'Waterloo', which in European languages takes the reader to a place with historical significance – without saying and explaining Napoleon? And when footnotes are the worst thing that can happen to a poem?

When Lín Zǐxiū writes that soldiers are pounding their oars against their boats, he is referring to a historical event, documented in a Tang Dynasty document, the Book of Jin. Soldiers, en route to a battle, beat their oars, vowing to reclaim lost territory. The phrase means 'unabashed determination', recognisable to readers of classical Chinese. I have aimed in scenarios like this to stay with the image, and to allow the image to work. Shengchi Hsu sent me incredible documents full of hyperlinks that offered literal translation, homophonic readings, visual and oral explanations, from which I have worked to make poems in English. We talked through the documents and the time difference between Manchester and Taichung, Shengchi responding to my questions with detailed answers. Though these are cast as co-translations, I'd prefer to think of them as collaborations between us. Shengchi has carried the heavier load.

Song of the Tigers in the Taiwan Mountains

by Qiū Féngjiǎ (1864–1912)

According to official histories,
there never were tigers in the mountains.
Now there are. But how?
Their existence defies imperial edict
and the laws of the Nine Heavens.
They range the mountains like jackals
or wolves, hunting and eating among
abandoned farmsteads and orchards.
These plots of land are overgrown
and uncared for. So-called savages had
settled there, building lives determined
not by the emperor but by belief –
people hidden in the mountains –
now threatened by predators.
Someone should inform the military,
but it must consider all outcomes.
Someone should pray to the gods
of the Yellow Springs, but the netherworld
is a cold, cold place. No. The fog will not lift.
I can offer only this song of lament
against tigers in the Taiwan mountains.

臺山有虎謠

丘逢甲 *(1864–1912)*

臺山乃無虎，
無虎古所傳。
臺山忽有虎，
有虎來何年。
上不從九天，
下不從九泉。
千百豺與狼，
擁之踞山巔。
山亦有民園，
山亦有民田。
田園已就蕪，
樵蘇且難前。
兇番據故巢，
出入乃晏然。
謂番命在天，
生殺非虎權。
翳彼山中民，
何獨垂饞涎。
上當告九天，
守閽恐有連。
下欲達九泉，
九泉何冥冥。
臺山瘴不開，
哀哉有虎篇。

The song of the difficult life

by Huáng Chúnqīng (1875–1956)

Life is difficult. Life in the village is difficult.
This is the song of the difficult life.

Soy pulp and sweet potatoes
– twice a day! – are all we eat.
To dread meal times, to survive
a decline in the price of sugar,
tea and rice worth so little.
Earnings are less than spending,
the gong sounds – rent must be paid,
no loans, many taxes. Everything
is sold off, even children. The house
is empty, the farms are empty.
Life in the village is difficult.

You did not foresee –
the untreated silk sold in Japan,
the grains of rice harvested early –
cutting strips from the heart
to bandage the wound.

農村難

黃純青 *(1875–1956)*

農村難，農村難，
農村之難良可嘆。

豆粕蕃薯日兩餐，
惡食不飽生存難。
甘蔗半價米茶賤，
利不及費維持難。
鑼聲入耳催租急，
告貸無門納稅難。
衣物典盡賣兒女，
債臺高築躲避難。
農村慘狀不忍看，
農村疲弊萬事難。
君不見 —

內地賣新絲，
臺灣糶新穀，
一例醫瘡剜心肉。

Three for Tokyo

by Lín Zīxiū (1880–1939)

Tsái, Jiǎng and Chén are resolved to leave for Tokyo,
resolved like ancient soldiers pounding oars on boats.
At their farewell, everyone is electrified –
Wang Wei's poem of Yangguan, someone quotes

it – but the outcome of this trip is uncertain,
like the *Kun Peng,* because the Japanese in their cruelty
are uncertain. The three cannot help crying.
They pour tears into the sea for their country.

送林培火 蔣渭水 陳逢源三君之京

林資修 *(1880–1939)*

一往情深是此行，
中流擊楫意難平。
風吹易水衝冠髮，
人唱陽關勸酒聲。

意外鯤鵬多變化，
眼中人獸漫縱橫。
臨歧一掬男兒淚，
願為同胞倒海傾。

Pomegranate Trees

by Lín Xiàntáng (1881–1956)

This afternoon their new branches are swaying in the breeze –
petals brighter than clouds, like dresses in the summer heat.

I envy them. They flower on a sunny day for good reason –
to compete with the redness of the sun.

石榴

林獻堂 *(1881–1956)*

牆畔柔枝舞午風，
羅裙妒殺火雲烘。

盛開夏日非無故，
欲與驕陽鬥孰紅。

Difficult to forget

by Cài Huìrú (1881–1929)

Here, the fields come to end against the sky
and the ten thousand things in my mind.
Down the road, there are willow trees,
weeping, and I am saddened with them –
until I think of the prison. At Qingshui Station,
people greet me, shake my hand,
fare me well to Taichung.
So many faces, brief and infinite.
It is good to see them.

Human warmth lasts longer than
mountains and rivers. And I am happy
to know my actions awakened a generation.
And I am happy even if I suffer.
Integrity – solid as pine or bamboo.
Heart – cast from stone and steel.
I could live in the tiger's mouth,
I could be myself, sleep there,
eat, and think of old Wén Tiānxiáng.
He never let up. His name is remembered.

意難忘

蔡惠如 *(1881–1929)*

芳草連空，
又千絲萬縷，
一路垂楊。
牽愁離故里，
壯氣入樊籠。
清水驛，
滿人叢，
握別到台中。
老輩青年齊見送，
感慰無窮。

山高水遠情長，
喜民心漸醒，
痛苦何妨。
松筠堅節操，
鐵石鑄心腸。
居虎口，
自雍容，
眠食亦如常。
記得當年文信國，
千古名揚。

The way we treat women

by Zhōu Dìngshān (1898–1975)

Women are very sad.
The ancients understood this:
better not born a woman
or all happiness and loneliness
are in someone else's control.
One evening, she welcomes her master
to bed. The next, she greets
the new concubine. Her life
is as bound as her feet:
there is no ignoring this.

Remember:
Banzhao – a woman – wrote history
and Xie Dàoyùn was a talented poet.
Is there a better story than that of Fa Mulan,
who joined the army in her father's place?

Remember too:
the freedoms they sing in the West
are sounding in Asia –
songs of equality and
an end to oppression.

This is the twentieth century
and women are hiding behind make-up
in their jade chambers,
turned away from the outside world.

The saddest are poor women.
They are seen as a burden.
Girls are sold to the wealthy
and as soon as they are gone
parents mourn, 'my child, my child,
the money you have earned
is a blessing!' They will never
recover. They hold themselves
and try not to cry.

My teeth go cold as I say this.
My hands shake as I write.
I want to be in the majority
and awaken all the others.
Where are those who agree,
who wish for equality?
And how did this come to pass?
Ah, it started with Lord Zhou's code of ethics.
If his wife was allowed to speak,
no oppressive voice would exist.

The world is full of terrible things.
The way we treat women is just one of them.

哀婦人

周定山 *(1898–1975)*

哀婦人，哀婦人，
古人言之頻。
人生莫作婦人身，
百年苦樂由他人。
今宵偶便東君面，
明朝難免痛迎新。
囚在深閨猶裹足，
非此不足謂天真。
君不見，
班昭纖手編漢史，
謝家清才能詠絮。
尚有堂堂花木蘭，
代父從征無雙譽。

又不見，
西歐唱自由，
次第灌輸入亞洲。
平權唱，
蹂躪休。
屑屑妝飾品，
日日躲玉樓。

不敢涉足社會上，
豈識廿紀之潮流。
傷心最是貧家女，
生活艱難終為累。
鬻身錢虜作婢姬，
一旦骨肉遽割棄，
聲聲吾兒莫悲啼，
倘得承恩多珠翠。

其實肝腸已碎如，
猶自甘言慰吞淚。
我云此事齒頻寒，
我寫此篇手頻顫。
恨不身化億萬千，
喚醒朦朧天下遍。
安得有心人奮起，
造成福同水平線。
問此伊誰是禍胎，
端由周公禮教開。
假使周婆能振起，
肯許束縛聲浪來。
世界滔滔事可哀，
豈特婦人問題而已哉。

Written in Response to Lín Xiàntáng's 'On the 228 Incident'

by Yè Róngzhōng (1900–1978)

'Brother' is a problematic word,
as two brothers can disagree.
One might argue that government oppressions
lessened when the protests began.

Where the other sees something is wrong,
even after the demonstrations:
that those who started the terror are free –
free and crowing like roosters.

敬步灌園先生二二八事件感懷瑤韻

葉榮鐘 *(1900–1978)*

莫漫逢人說弟兄，
鬩牆貽笑最傷情。
予求予取擅威服，
如火如荼方震驚。

浩浩輿情歸寂寞，
重重疑案未分明。
巨奸禍首傳無恙，
法外優遊得意鳴。

Female Students 1930

by Huáng Jīnchuān (1907–1990)

How is it possible to bury one's head
in a bedroom when I could carry

books to Tokyo? I see a female sparrow
crouched low – the male is flying.

Books are more than material things
and learning is slow, necessary work.

Will female and male never be equal?
Will my learning go to waste?

女學生

黃金川 *(1907–1990)*

詎甘繡閣久埋頭，
負笈京師萬里遊。

雌伏胸愁無點墨，
雄飛跡可遍寰球。

書深莫被文明誤，
學苦須從哲理求。

安得女權平等日，
漫將天賦付東流。

The Taiwan Spirit

SHENGCHI HSU

'Would you be interested in translating some classical Chinese poetry from Taiwan?' the translation project coordinator at the National Museum of Taiwan Literature asked. Translation? I found little reason to say no. After all, that's what I have studied and been learning to do for several years. But 'classical Chinese poetry from Taiwan'? – A long pause… I vaguely remembered the name *Lìshè* 櫟社, a poetry club founded at the start of the twentieth century, based in the infamously grand Lin Family Ancestral Residence on the outskirts of my home city of Taichung. I could not recall reading their poetry. I felt ashamed and embarrassed: *was there ever any classical Chinese poetry produced in Taiwan?* But I did, in the end, accept the invitation.

I started to look into classical Taiwanese poetry in a library nearby: six recently-compiled volumes of poems by a handful of poets whose names rang no bells. There were a couple of other smaller collections with annotations. The scarcity of published material was disturbing, and even more so my ignorance. The poems in these collections take the forms of classical Han Chinese poetry: *lǜshī* 律詩, *juéjù* 絕句, *cí* 詞, etc., reminding me of poets from ancient Chinese dynasties, such as Li Po and Bai Jüyi, whose works I had been made to memorise. I recognised a handful of poets, primarily for their socio-historic significance rather than their literary achievement, but a large majority of the them, including many with Japanese names, were unfamiliar. Why would

I – a reasonably well-educated Taiwanese man in his forties – not have been aware of poems like these produced in Taiwan by poets from Taiwan? Were they not as significant as the ancient Chinese poems? Why were they missing from my education?

The absence speaks volumes about Taiwan's history. As a child growing up in the 1980s and 1990s I experienced Taiwan's transformation. Cities boomed; cars and scooters jammed the streets, and it was every child's dream to eat at McDonald's, Hardee's or Wendy's. As well as the economic boom, the lifting of martial law in Taiwan in 1987 was a giant leap towards democracy, and I felt its effects at school. I was no longer forced to speak Mandarin, nor would I be fined five *yuan* for speaking my parents' once-considered-vulgar Taiwanese dialect. I no longer had to bow to General Chiang's portrait and vow to 'recover the lost Mainland and save our compatriots' at the start of every lesson. There was little change, however, in what and how I was learning: Li Po, Wang Wei and Du Fu, as well as many other writers of historical significance in China kept dominating the pages in my Chinese language textbooks, and we continued to learn every piece by heart. Their languages sounded so alien, and having to memorise how to turn them into the modern tongue murdered any pleasure in them. My school learning was as regimental as ever, much like those stiff military police standing guard over their camp near my school.

I spent those years in compulsory education, cramming works of ancient poets who lived thousands of miles away in DàLù, literally Big Land, or the Mainland as they called it. That education to me was the government's attempt to tell school kids that China and Taiwan were inseparable, even with the differences in political ideologies between the two entities. Culture – the arts, literature, music, customs, traditions – was possibly the government's final hope to keep the China–Taiwan family bond intact. There was nothing wrong with that, as there is no denying that Taiwan inherits and preserves many Chinese cultural characteristics. But the government's prioritisation of classical literature from the other side of the Taiwan Straits left no opportunity for me, and my contemporaries, to discover literary works from Taiwan. They were erased from the curriculum as though they had never existed.

It's sad but true that Taiwan and its classical Chinese poetry seem to have a similar fate. Taiwan has been overlooked and erased internationally. Its absence resembles that of classical Chinese poetry throughout my schooling: people around the globe are deprived of the opportunity to learn about Taiwan. No wonder many still mistake Taiwan for Thailand, and vice versa.

Taiwan's absence from the international arena has not, however, silenced its poetry. Taiwan has fought its way through numerous setbacks, against international pressures, to make its voice heard. This voice – of protest, resistance and resilience – perhaps best exemplifies what we locals call the 'Taiwan Spirit'. It is an uncompromising voice that speaks up for those living on the margins of societies and against unfairness and injustice. It is a voice born of Taiwanese peoples' need to survive and be recognised. From Chiu Fengjia's allegorical criticism of the Qing government's failing policy of 'Opening up Taiwan's Mountains and Pacifying Indigenous Peoples' (1847) that caused ethnic conflicts in Taiwan, to Lin Zixiu's and Tzai Huiru's retelling of Taiwanese intellectuals' fights against Japanese colonialism, and Yeh Rongzong's doubts about the 'truth' of the bloody 228 incident in 1947, these poets provided firsthand accounts of significant events in Taiwan's history of democratisation, undeterred by fear of the authorities of their times. Meanwhile, Huang Chunqing's lament about poverty in Taiwan's farming communities further illuminates the challenging living conditions and unfair treatment people received under Japanese rule (1885–1945). As well as criticism of government authority, poets like Zhou Dingshan and Huang Jinchuan also provide social critiques of the longstanding gender inequality in Taiwan in the early twentieth century. As male and female poet respectively, they wrote towards the day when gender equality could be achieved in Taiwan. Lin Xiantang's punchy poem uses the pomegranate flowers under the scorching sun to sketch out Taiwan's unwillingness to succumb to pressure and affirms the Taiwan Spirit.

I returned to Taiwan after nearly two decades in the United Kingdom. Picking up these worn collections and criticisms of classical Chinese poetry from Taiwan, I feel like a school child once again. But this time there is no rote learning, nor am I reading these poems for an exam. I am experiencing the *pleasure* of reading poetry that was lost in my pressure-cooker education. In the meantime, through reading these poems, I am learning about the parts of Taiwan's history that people did not dare mention for many years. And, working with Evan Jones, I have the chance to share these poems through translation with anglophone readers around the world, to help our voice be heard.

Reviews

Aping the Original

Colin Burrows, *Imitating Authors* (OUP) £46.49
Reviewed by Geoffrey Heptonstall

The question is stated simply: 'How do human beings learn sophisticated usage of language from others, and yet end up sounding like themselves?' The answer is long. It is unending, according to Ben Jonson (whose observation begins the enquiry).

Where, then, may we begin? The beginning is in antiquity. What has been written over the centuries, however original the perception and expression, is part of an ancient tradition. We write for the future while looking to the past. An obvious example is Shakespeare, who was rarely if ever the first to write on a theme. But he wrote in a manner that was his alone – until, of course, others followed.

We learn how to live by copying our mentors, filtering that mimesis through our personal approach. A good mimic may not be a good actor. To act or to write well is to be oneself even in another person's voice.

Colin Burrows is guided in his enquiry by the Latin rhetorical device *imitatio*, a word with multiple meanings. The formal and the adaptive uses of *imitatio* seem the most relevant to modern (that is, post-Renaissance) usage. It is partly a question of style. Formal imitation absorbs the manner, including the vocabulary, of the original. The adaptive mode concerns what Dr Burrows calls 'practical transformation', meaning the absorption of certain authorial characteristics so that they become habitual to another writer.

This seems to differ from influence by the close relation between the existing model and its imitation. On the other hand, we are not considering plagiarism where the imitating author directly transfers a created work without any process of development.

The practice of imitation is a learning skill. The tyro acquires a personal style by an initial mimesis of other writers (a habit which Plato condemned as morally questionable). Plato's doubts about poetry, as Burrows illustrates, are founded on a failure to understand how an author in maturity goes beyond mimesis to authentic creation.

Authors learn from those who have gone before, though not always in terms of acceptance. A different perspective may be expressed. This is more than a question of style. A slight shift in emphasis may change the nature of an enterprise.

Even the act of replication involves a transformation, Burrows argues. We feel intuitively that a copy must differ in some degree from the original. Here one may cite the Borges story *Pierre Menard, Author of the Quixote*. The eponymous Menard rewrites *Don Quixote* in a word-for-word copying of the original. But words change their meaning, and often our understandings differ vastly from those of Cervantes.

Of course the story is a conceit, but there is a genuine challenge to our presumptions about creation and authorship. Am I reading a poem, or is the poem reading me? By this I mean that the act of reading can be, ought to be, a transformative process. I can recall the poem's lines. I impress them in my mind and rewrite them in my future responses. I quote a line but not perfectly, for I have made it mine.

We may leave the last word to Quintilian, a key witness in Burrows's enquiry. For Quintilian it is the *vis*, the spark of originality that makes a literary creation. Whatever debts must be paid to others, that spark, so elusive that it evades definition, is the essence. Mary Shelley, steeped in the natural histories of classical authors, created a monstrous imitation of a human being. This raises questions not easily asked, and perhaps unanswerable. What spark, Dr Burrows wonders, illuminated Mary Shelley's mind? A gift from the gods, perhaps?

Poet's Prose

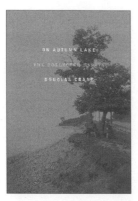

Douglas Crase, *On Autumn Lake: The Collected Essays*
(Nightboat Editions) £16.99
Carl Phillips, *My Trade Is Mystery* (Yale University Press)
£15.49
Reviewed by Ian Pople

In his trademark, graceful prose, Douglas Crase makes the following comment in his review of *The Complete Prose of Marianne Moore*, 'To regard the prose as primarily a concordance, however, or a life, would be to imply that a poet's prose is only ancillary to the poetry'. What is so typical of Crase's prose is not simply the comment as a whole, which we can come back to, but the use of the word 'concordance', coupled as it is with 'life' and 'ancillary'. Crase, who spent his professional life as a speech writer, knows exactly what it means to put such vocabulary into the air, as it were. Although poets as a breed might be seen as choosing their words with care, there is something utterly exquisite about the precision of the words I've picked out above. For one thing, to suggest that the poet's prose is a concordance or, even, a life, and yet is ancillary is to make a rather strange claim. It is to state that the prose is a kind of reference to themes in the poems, and, almost, a life that the poetry is not. Life, here, is 'ancillary', additional or extra to the poems. But the sentence actually tells us that the prose is none of these things, or rather that the prose and the poetry are, as Crase comments just below this, 'not even separable. Criticism, [Moore] wrote, inspires creation.' This Crase follows up with 'No surprise, then, to find it as recalcitrant as the poetry.'

Carl Phillips's essays have often dealt with that sense of recalcitrance. His first volume of essays, *Coin of the Realm*, begins with an essay called 'The Case for Beauty'. It begins: 'Beauty, at least when it is referred to by that name – suffers the same treatment by too many contemporary poets as does authority in poetry. It gets dismissed as naïve, or irrelevant, or somehow on the wrong side of the field on whose *other* side we are all assumed to have happily set up camp together.' What seems to be recalcitrant here is part of the very nature of making. And the recalcitrance of the nature of making is what Phillips has often returned to in his two recent books of essays. In his previous book, *The Art of Daring,* Phillips asked us to use the restlessness of imagination coupled with 'that daring that can bring us – loss and brokenness in tow – to unknowing'.

Those elements of recalcitrance in the imagination leading to unknowing are clearly present in Phillips's new collection of essays, whose title *My Trade Is Mystery* pulls together those previous concerns. In addition, the title plays on the word 'trade' and its associations with not only commerce but also a sense of exchange, the 'life' and the 'art', perhaps; although Phillips does demur from this in his introduction. The book is written for and dedicated to his students and contains seven sections from whose titles we can gather the emphases of the book. They are: Ambition, Stamina, Silence, Politics, Practice, Audience and Community. As Phillips himself puts it, this is 'a book in which I told my students what I thought they might most need to know, not in terms of how to write or how to be a writer, but in terms of how to live *as* a writer'. Phillips calls these sections 'meditations'.

It would be tempting to suggest that *My Trade Is Mystery* is a kind of poetry self-help book. The thing that prevents this is Phillips's sheer emotional intelligence – an attribute which underpins his poetry, too. But here it means that the sections are deepened and have more resonance. What is important to Phillips is that the terms he uses are defined properly, and for him that means teasing out how such terms work within an artistic life. In his section on 'Ambition', for example, he first asserts the sense of vocation for the writer. Within that, he comments that ambition may feel out of place, but the kinds of ambition he is suggesting are 'an ambition for the work – the art – to capture what can't be captured otherwise, and even then can't be captured entirely; which is to say, defeat is built into the mechanism'. Phillips goes on to exemplify this by writing about the idea of the love poem. At first the love poem is joyful, then the relationship fails. So the poet writes a new poem, and so forth. This, Phillips states, means that not only have the relationships changed, but love and the self have changed as well. It is this type of teasing out and exemplifying that make *My Trade Is Mystery* much more than a self-help book, and elevate it to a rounded exploration of what it means to take writing into a life.

Douglas Crase begins his collected essays by stating that 'if there's anything to explain about this book it's that I never planned to write criticism and, no matter the appearance of the pages that follow, I never did'. Thus, he goes on to say, the essays 'are appreciations or predilections, though to be truthful they were more like affairs of the heart, affairs of attention and intellectual desire, rather than criticism'. As I observed before, Crase's manner is always towards a graceful self-deprecation.

But Crase is right to suggest that these essays are more than criticism. For a start, a number of these pieces are often part memoir, part criticism, particularly but not wholly of figures from the New York School, many of whom Crase knew personally. Thus, Crase can begin his essay 'A Voice Like the Day' with 'Because my name appears in his poem "Dining Out with Doug and Frank," I should probably disclose that James Schuyler was a friend of mine – though of the two of us, Doug and Frank [Polach, Douglas Crase's husband], it was Frank he really liked'. Crase can then say that 'people who never saw the three of us together sometimes nervously suggest that "Dining Out with Doug and Frank" betrays a[n] amusement at my expense. They do not need to be embarrassed. James Schuyler was arguably the most perceptive observer I knew, in person or in poetry, but it was perception without malice.'

What the essay then does is weave quite effortlessly between reminiscence and Crase's own perceptive take on the poetry. Crase points out that in Schuyler's book *The Morning of the Poem,* there was very little use of 'like' or 'as'. Crase later comments, 'When [Schuyler] does arrive on an analogy it is not the subject-to-subject kind that William James derided as bare likeness: it is the kind that slips its reader from the subject to a surprisingly apposite, on-the-move event. "March is here / like a granny / a child doesn't / like to kiss".' In this lightly driven sentence, there are a number of things happening. The first is the reference to the literary criticism of William James; Crase's learning here is both exactly and lightly worn, with its inflection of 'derided'. The second is a sense of Crase's moving both with and against William James. Here, it is Crase's sense of the vehicle, to use I.A. Richards's terminology, in this case 'a granny a child doesn't like to kiss'. Crase sees that Schuyler is himself, involving the reader in the trajectory of the poem. Elsewhere *On Autumn Lake* collects Crase's equally perceptive and precise essays on a range of subjects – from Lorine Niedecker to a history of the Tibor de Nagy Gallery in New York, from Crase's great hero, Emerson, to the painter Robert Dash.

The Muirs

Margery Palmer McCulloch, *Edwin and Willa Muir: A Literary Marriage* (OUP) £100
Reviewed by Andrew Hadfield

Edwin Muir (1887–1959) was well known and celebrated in his lifetime. Championed by T.S. Eliot, he had his collected and selected poems published by Faber, he was awarded the CBE, he wrote scores of reviews for highbrow journals and published many other works, including a well-received autobiography, as well as some novels. Willa Muir, née Anderson (1890–1970), although – more or less – content to play second fiddle to her poetic husband, was also a formidable and prolific writer. She produced two novels, and probably could and should have written a lot more, as well as a range of

critical essays on women and on Scottish identity. Together – though it was really Willa who was the driving force – they translated a number of modernist German writers, most famously Franz Kafka, in editions that have only recently been replaced.

Lives

Edwin was born on Orkney, and had a happy early childhood, before his family was forced to move, first to a less successful farm on a neighbouring island and then to Glasgow. Taking various disagreeable clerical jobs, he was rescued when he met Willa Anderson soon after the First World War. Willa had grown up in Montrose, on the Scottish east coast, but her family were originally from the Shetlands, and the dialect of those islands was spoken at home. Like Edwin, she was conscious of being both Scots and an outsider. She had graduated with a first-class degree in Modern Languages at St. Andrews, one of the first Scottish women to have such a successful undergraduate career. She gave up her position as assistant principal at a teacher training college and persuaded her new husband to be bold, and together they moved to Prague. For both, it was a spectacular adventure that set a pattern for the rest of their lives.

From Prague they moved on to Dresden, conscious that Willa's health, never good at the best of times, might require a dryer and warmer place. Both had a fashionable interest in psychology, especially dreams, and were immersing themselves in psychoanalytic writings, as well as literature, as their fluency in German improved. Edwin was obsessed with recording and analysing his dreams, and his autobiography is stuffed with them, often at the expense of actual events. In the early 1920s, the couple travelled between Germany, Austria and Italy, returned to London, went off to Scotland and to St. Tropez, then to a fishing village with a population of itinerant bohemian intellectuals, and to Menton, where they were especially happy. Like many couples, the Muirs had minor disagreements in their early years together. Willa found Edwin's friendship with the larger-than-life John Holms (1897–1934), later the partner of Peggy Guggenheim (1897–1979), something of a trial. Edwin often paid fulsome tribute to Holms in his letters, and he appears as a major influence in the autobiography, even though Holms never managed to finish the *magnum opus* that occupied his speech if not his thoughts before his untimely death.

When Willa became pregnant, the couple sought to establish themselves with a place of their own. They eventually settled in the quiet East Sussex town of Crowborough. Feeling isolated from literary life they returned to London in the early 1930s, frequently visiting Eastern Europe through their involvement in the writers' organisation, PEN International. After their son, Gavin, was knocked over by an oil tanker and had to spend time in hospital recovering from a broken leg, the family decided to return to Scotland.

Initially they went to Orkney, then to St. Andrews, the move marking the increasing importance of Scotland in their writings. They were close to the major writers Christopher Murray Grieve (Hugh MacDiarmid) and

James Leslie Mitchell (Lewis Grassic Gibbon). These friendships were often as fractious as they were fulfilling, Grieve disapproving of what he saw as the Muirs' tepid socialism and lack of desire for real social change. In turn, Edwin was critical of Grieve's commitment to Scots dialect in his writing, and his public comments caused something of a split, even though he had recognised the impressive achievement of MacDiarmid's *A Drunk Man Looks at the Thistle* (1926). Both Edwin and Willa were upset by Gibbon's premature death at the age of thirty-four in 1935, when a doctor failed to realise that peritonitis had set in after an operation for a gastric ulcer.

Staying in St. Andrews, the Muirs continued to translate German literature, which was much in demand until the outbreak of war, making occasional visits to the continent, and so developing their sense of Scottish and European literary identities. Willa's health was proving ever more of a worry, and friends and acquaintances who saw her only sporadically were often shocked by her haggard appearance. So that they could be together the family moved to Edinburgh, where Edwin was now working for the British Council. While St. Andrews, like Crowborough, had left them somewhat isolated but with time for writing, Edwin, who also had his health issues, was now overwhelmed by the number of people he was expected to meet. The latter half of the Second World War perhaps saw Edwin's closest involvement in debates about poetry and poetics. At the same time, he was also writing a significant quantity of verse as well as reviewing as assiduously as ever.

Their wanderlust renewed after the war, the Muirs asked to return to their first city of exile, Prague. Hoping to play a small part in rebuilding the cultural life of the city, Edwin accepted the directorship of the British Council there. Hardly surprisingly, Soviet-occupied Prague at the start of the Cold War proved a different prospect to the liberating city they had lived in twenty-five years earlier. PEN International meetings were fraught, with leading figures in the organisation urging reconciliation with the former German occupiers, while many ordinary Czechs felt that it was far too early to forgive and forget. At one meeting a woman ran out and returned with a blood-stained shirt that had pieces of torn skin attached to it. The shirt had belonged to her husband, the head of an underground group who had sent information to Britain, and the Gestapo sent it to her after they had tortured and killed him. One of Edwin's better-known poems, 'The Good Town', was written during this period, reflecting on a sullied, paranoid city that had suffered at the hands of both Nazis and communists.

The next two years were spent in Rome, after which the Muirs moved on to Newbattle Abbey in the Edinburgh suburbs, a residential adult education college whose director Edwin became. Willa, dogged by now debilitating ill health, was gaining a reputation for unpredictability and waspishness, one reason why she never received the recognition she deserved in her lifetime. Furthermore, Gavin was proving to be a troubled young man, and he seems to have had an especially difficult relationship with his extremely forthright mother. Although Edwin and Willa provided support and found

his failure to gain entrance to music college incomprehensible, more independent witnesses felt that his piano playing was over-loud and somewhat limited.

Edwin was offered the poetry professorship at Harvard in 1955, and the Muirs were able to escape across the Atlantic, back into a more literary and academic world. They found American freedoms exhilarating – Willa in particular was enjoying social occasions in which women were not seen as merely appendages of their partners, but where their opinions were actively sought. On their return they bought a cottage in the centre of the Cambridgeshire village Swaffham Prior. Gavin lived with them and was proving ever more of a worry, unable to find employment and spending his time striding over the moors, or playing the piano – loudly and badly – at a neighbour's house, not helped by his now diagnosed deafness. Edwin was still producing poetry, including his best-loved poem, 'The Horses', written against the backdrop of the fear of nuclear destruction.

By now neither Willa nor Edwin was in the best of health. Edwin was suffering from heart failure and, as his critical reputation reached its zenith, he died, in January 1959. Willa lived on for just over another decade, determined, as she put it in a letter to an old friend, 'to recover my old self... and be like the woman [Edwin] fell in love with forty years ago'. She wrote two extended essays on women and culture in Scotland, *Women: An Inquiry* and *Mrs. Grundy in Scotland*. Both are interesting rather than successful pieces, making extensive use of her knowledge of psychology, championing creative expression and freedom, and lamenting the undue influence of puritanical religion in Scottish society. However, as McCulloch notes, 'the intellectually discursive or ironically polemical essay was not her best medium' and, as in the past, Willa struggled to find publishers for her work.

In the spring of 1964 a series of programmes on Radio 3 explored Edwin's life and writing, the final one recording Willa's memories and reflections on her husband. A rather tart review by Arthur Calder-Marshall in *The Listener* complained that when he visited them in Hampstead, he found that Willa was obscuring and smothering Edwin. McCulloch sees this as a common misconception of the nature of their relationship. While Willa tended to be 'extravagantly loquacious in public', she was not a domineering figure, but 'very dependent upon Edwin in their private life', even though appearances tended to misrepresent the balance of the couple's existence. Willa still harboured literary ambitions, writing to Kathleen Raine, a constant friend who had shepherded her through a pain-ridden old age, that she thought she '*might* get a small book done' [emphasis in original]. But she died in May 1970 without having produced one. The obituaries were respectful and drew attention to her achievements as an independent woman at a time when there was little encouragement for bold, intelligent, unconventional female writers.

Willa

It is surely a shame that Willa lacked confidence in her novel writing, as her two novels are both challenging accounts of complicated women who wrestle with the limitations of provincial life in good and bad ways. *Imagined Corners* (1919) charts the self discovery of a young woman, Elizabeth, who grows up in Calderwick, a fictionalised version of Montrose, where Willa spent her childhood. Elizabeth has to learn that a successful union requires more than youthful passion, and after a protracted series of quarrels with her husband, Hector, she begins a journey to find herself. Calderwick contains several different women, who represent, according to McCulloch, 'stages in the author's own journey to maturity', and the novel is structured around the contrasts between them. Elizabeth is clever but inexperienced, and she stands in contrast to her sister-in-law, Elise, the widow of a German scholar, who has returned to her hometown to rediscover her younger self and identity. As is obvious from even the barest details, the novel is ambitious in its plotting and deployment of themes. Willa was thinking through her complex relationship to Scottish provincial life; making use of her knowledge of multi-layered European fiction, as well as English modernist styles and techniques; looking back to experimental pioneers such as George Eliot; and foregrounding her interest in psychoanalysis.

McCulloch thinks quite highly of the novel, but to some readers – me being one of them – it looks like a rather messy experiment. The second novel, *Mrs. Ritchie* (1933) gets much shorter shrift, and Willa felt that she lost her way in that novel. Certainly, it is much simpler in plot, telling the story of the monstrous Mrs. Ritchie, also of Calderwood, a relentlessly Calvinist bigot who inflicts misery on everyone she encounters, driving her husband to an early grave, her shell-shocked son to suicide and her daughter to flee at the end of the novel as the two women visit the cemetery to lay flowers on the graves of their menfolk. Even so, *Mrs. Ritchie* is a powerful work of gothic fiction. Its protagonist is transformed from an intelligent young girl, her chance to be a teacher thwarted by impoverished, unimaginative parents, to a psychotic pleasure-hating monster. Mrs. Ritchie takes the self-denying logic of the kirk to an insane conclusion. She does not merely deny her increasingly bewildered and hostile children such minor creature comforts as parties, but she openly laments their growing up because she can no longer beat them for their sins, and, they will now need to avoid life's temptations if they are to get into heaven when they die. There is surely wonderful dark comedy in Mrs. Ritchie's constant refrain that she has been a self-sacrificing saint throughout her life, and she spends the latter stages of the novel pretending to be deaf after her son hits her, a malevolent presence who reminds her family that God does not want the wicked to be happy. *Mrs. Ritchie* raises a series of significant issues – perversity, as in the case of the main character, is often the result of distorted ambitions, and small-town provincial life can be as miserable as sin – but it can never simply be reduced to them.

It is also good to remember what a fine, idiomatic translator Willa was. The opening of Kafka's *The Trial*, which appeared in 1925, the same year as her novel, surely reads as well as the original:

Someone must have been telling lies about Joseph K., for without having done anything wrong he was arrested one fine morning. His landlady's cook, who always brought him his breakfast at eight o'clock, failed to appear on this occasion. That had never happened before. K. waited for a little while longer, watching from his pillow the old lady opposite, who seemed to be peering at him with a curiosity unusual even for her, but then, feeling both put out and hungry, he rang the bell.

These sentences capture the weird sense of menace and ordinariness of Kafka's original, one non-event leading the protagonist to worry that nothing is quite right even though little seems to have changed. It is hard to see that more recent translations mark a significant improvement, and the surface blandness of Willa's translation has set the standard for what has followed.

Edwin

Edwin's reputation as poet – and, perhaps, novelist – would seem to be secure. Like Willa, he was heavily indebted to psychoanalysis, and what is probably his best novel, *The Marionette* (1927), tells the story of a young boy with learning difficulties living with his father in a Salzburg suburb, struggling to make sense of the world. This he can only do through his obsession with puppets, dolls that simultaneously enable and hinder him. Like Eliot and Yeats, Edwin had an eye for telling, demotic phrases of great power and resonance. 'The Child Dying', for example, concludes with the line 'I did not know death was so strange'. Slightly too disturbing – even Kafkaesque – to be a funeral staple, it nevertheless has spiritual resonances that have struck a chord with many readers over the years. Indeed, a number of Edwin's most characteristic lyric passages depend on a sense of the uncanny, expressed by a sudden twist. 'The Horses' seems like a gloomy poem with the destruction of the mechanised world and grim sights of a warship, 'heading north, / Dead bodies piled up on the deck', when suddenly 'the strange horses' appear, a quasi-religious moment that signals 'Our life is changed; their coming, our beginning'.

His experience of antisemitism in 1920s Austria, when even nice, sensible, educated people explained the nature of the 'Jewish problem' to their bewildered guests, and the grim reality of life in Cold War Prague, left its mark on several poems. In the ballad (a form that Edwin especially enjoyed) 'The Castle', the inhabitants of an unnamed fortress complacently imagine that they are safe, before they are undone by a 'wizened warder' who lets their enemies in through a small, unnoticed gate. Consequently

    our maze of tunnelled stone
Grew thin and treacherous as air.
The cause was lost without a groan,
The famous citadel overthrown,
And all its secret galleries bare.

Many of Edwin's poems express the fear that beneath a surface harmony lurks terrible danger (just as in his more optimistic poems there is the sense of a sudden reversal of fortune). In 'The Good Town', the speaker looks at the rubble of a once-great city and laments its tragic destruction. After various wars and disasters the people he knows have become 'the frightened faces / Peeping round corners, secret police, informers', and he has to ask, 'Could it have come from us? Was our peace peace? / Our goodness goodness?', again using ordinary speech to indicate the sinister ways in which language has been corrupted without anyone paying quite enough attention to be able to stop it. At other times, the repeated actions of the everyday work to head off disaster, as in 'The Return of Odysseus', in which Penelope's hope against hope that order will be restored as she weaves and undoes her tapestry to ward off the suitors, is about to be realised because 'even then Odysseus on the long / And winding road of the world was on his way'.

The Book
Edwin & Willa Muir is an informative and interesting joint biography, which, sadly, its author did not live to see, the work having been completed by the poet and academic Roderick Watson. I sometimes would have liked a bit more on the literary works themselves, as the analysis and judgements can be a bit perfunctory, and it is not as if there is a plethora of critical work on the Muirs, but that is often the way with biographies. The book succeeds in outlining why they both matter, and the significant links that they were instrumental in forging between rural Scotland and metropolitan, modernist Europe. In particular, it rescues Willa Muir, and demonstrates that she deserves far more credit as a translator and novelist than she has been given, and that her sacrifice in supporting her husband's career at the expense of her own should not be taken quite at face value.

Lyric Synthesis

Lucy Mercer, *Emblem* (Prototype) £12.00
Karenjit Sandhu, *young girls!* (the87press) £10.00
Reviewed by Kate Simpson

During the late Renaissance, the Italian scholar and jurist Andrea Alciato began writing what is now commonly accepted as the first 'emblem book'. *Emblematum liber* (originally released in 1531 with woodcuts by the German publisher and illustrator Heinrich Steiner) comprised a series of poems framed with a kind of 'dec-

orative inlay', 'inserted' illustrations, and mottos. In these innovative leaves, image and text came together in a kind of interrelated mimesis, in the process inventing the emblem publication as a whole new cultural genre, widely popularised as a 'humanist pastime' across Europe.

It feels as counterintuitive to introduce a book review with such specific social and historical context as it does to imbue the reading process with the events of a poet's life – the beauty of poetry existing, implicitly, as an unrestricted, liberal space, vehemently open to interpretation. However, it is in this precise milieu that Lucy Mercer's debut collection, *Emblem*, exists, intentionally creating a dialogue between past and present, creator and creation, publication and interpretation. In her preface, Mercer states that she came across Alciato's book whilst pregnant with her son. The emblems' constructed worlds – and their layered abstraction – perhaps mimicked the ways her own body was becoming a hybrid framework, one body 'inserted' within another. Context is placed centre stage throughout the collection, as when the speaker states: 'I am here / in the poem too its rings of rock so carefully / winding through one another.' ('Phantasias')

Here, emblems, like pregnant bodies, are filled with duplicities: messages within messages, lives within lives like Matryoshka dolls: 'your red historic feathers / coming out of my body / in histrionics / covering my eyes / and my other eyes / and my mother's eyes' ('Mother'). Akin to the inception of the emblem and its various re-interpretations, the speaker's body is growing and mutating, creating something 'new' whilst being transposed in the process:

> In labour, on all fours changing
> what is elsewhere for what is here
> the body casts vomit onto the floor
>
> The mind images it is drowning
> eye-high muddy Ocean, two buoys
> floating on the rising rows
>
> Forever watching the cinematic
> threshing-floor of its own inquisition,
> this mind that is the body's idea –
>   ('Single Mothers Study Metaphysics')

Throughout, Mercer commits to obscurity. Scarlet fever, hydrangeas, torches, cats and cowboys share space with apples, doppelgängers and alphabets whilst the axes constantly shift, and certainties are made uncertain. Objects frequently dissolve and colours swap places, whilst bodies are 'undressed' by salt to reveal their 'uninfinite holes' ('Zero'), and anonymous figures are cast as 'spilled [people] resting in wet lines' ('Woodcut Print'). The self, Mercer tells us, is permeable and porous to meaning, whilst the truth of all other forms – living or non-living – is a matter of perception, interchangeable and shape-shifting:

> at last you decide
> on the red rose

and you eat it

at last you decide
on the green rose
and you eat it

one is called text
and the other, image.
('Ten Shifts')

Through rigorous research into the emblematic form, Mercer has crafted a deeply considered and self-reflexive collection that is as close to critical theory as it is poetry – considering the ways that various messages take shape and resonate with their recipients, however literal or abstract. Whether it's genetic codes passed from parent to child, mottos passed on to future generations through printed publications, or visual information carried along the optic nerve, modes of communication are constructed and deconstructed. *Emblem* is a multi-dimensional masterpiece, and offers profundity with every page.

In similar ways, Karenjit Sandhu's *young girls!* sparks conversations between past and present, and between different interpersonal contexts. Just as Mercer's twenty-first century mother breathes life into the work of a sixteenth-century writer, this sumptuous, sometimes saccharine collection 'reimagines' the life of the twentieth-century painter Amrita Sher-Gil through the lens of 1990s girlhood, conjuring post-Impressionist palettes amid scrunchies, bras, calico shells, flares and Angel Delight.

Throughout, Sandhu focuses heavily on the limbic system and its nostalgic capacities, the speaker re-accessing moments with vivid detail. The collection maintains a feeling of heady sensory stimulation, particularly through lingering scents: 'jelly, petrol thickened and smelling of soap' ('Jelly's Fugitive'); 'pickled mangoes / forgotten, sour, winking discontent' ('Hiding in your neighbour's rasoee'). Candyfloss and sugar are frequently called into play, and a sense of sweetness both cloying and heavy is sustained until stomachs eventually turn:

We walked past the fairground in '94 and a woman in
    a sari,
she gave us a bag of candy floss

a prickly fizz on the tip of my tongue
as I watched her in purple, move

you ate nothing and you said nothing,
apparently you gave up sugar in '92

crowds swallowed you, whole
I belched, and vomited onto my jelly sandals.
('Sick')

Sandhu explores the ways girls test their growing bodies, searching for pleasure and finding its limits, experiencing softness as well as the 'sharp lines' of their own existence. Burns and bruises are frequent. Bodies, letters and

fruits are held in comparison, each filled with possibility and vulnerability – easy to damage, to be consumed or to be filled with rapture. Colours, too, are integral: burnt ochre, peacock and Prussian blues are weaved into the balmy vignettes, 'globbed' onto the page generously amongst various canonical references. While Sher-Gil – and the 'young girls' – are never named, Cézanne, Gauguin, Matisse and Duchamp are mentioned generously, overshadowing the women, but never their experiences:

On the bus route home, he thundered upstairs blotchy and red. Red, and blue on the inside, but not lost. So much fruit, his ripened cherries squished and bleeding, red. Stuffed into his side, back and front pockets of his double-breasted dress coat and trousers of fine wool. He sat in the seat directly in front of me and I could see the back of his neck, yellow. Stripes of orange from the city's August sun. I wanted to say something like, can I give you a bag for your cherries?

('on a bus with Paul Cézanne')

The collection maintains a disarmingly relaxed register, almost diaristic, which feels authentic to its youthful speakers, navigating an explosion of visual, tactile and gustatory information, and soupy hormones. Meanwhile, through a bold and animated use of ekphrasis, Sandhu replicates the ways our minds sort through information to determine what will remain – in the memory and on the page – ready to be accessed, re-accessed and re-interpreted, by ourselves, or indeed, someone else.

Wounds of Exile

Olivia Elias, *Chaos, Crossing*, translated from the French by Kareem James Abu-Zeid (World Poetry Books) $20
Reviewed by Ali Al-Jamri

Chaos, Crossing is the first book of Olivia Elias's poetry in English. The Palestinian poet is of the Nakba generation: born in Haifa in 1944, she was four when her family and nation were made refugees and expelled from their land. While technically a translation of her French-language 2019 collection *Chaos, Traversée,* the book includes two poems from her 2015 and 2017 collections and some twenty-five poems written since 2019. Elias and her translator have restructured the collection, and this edition includes the new poems in both French and English for the first time, such that there will be things here new to any French reader already familiar with Elias's work.

The collection, arranged across four sections, takes us through visions of occupation, exile, aftermath, compassion and power. The first part is powerfully prophetic, declaiming the rage of Palestine in 'Flames of Fire': 'I was born / in this / seismic time / that engulfed / even the name / of my father / and his father's father'.

This gives way to the more dystopian second part, ushered in with 'In the Kingdom of Bosch and Orwell' which portrays Gaza: 'forbidden sky / forbidden sea / *no exit*'. While Palestine is at the core, Elias's compassion is not just national. 'Mediterranean II' takes us to Lampedusa, recalling both the Italian-run refugee camp there and the tragic and avoidable drowning of hundreds on the same-named ship *Lampedusa*: 'How could I forget your oceanic / trenches now turned into cemeteries?' Her poignant poems 'I Say Your Name' and 'I Say Your, Their Names' recall 'George Floyd the giant'.

The third part deals primarily with exile, as in 'Other Name', which through metaphor and allusion deconstructs the very word 'exile'. The aftermaths of conflicts are gendered, as so often it is women left to pick up the pieces after the destruction men caused. In the third part, I hear echoes of the empathy and wit of that other poet of aftermaths, Wisława Szymborska, particularly in a poem like 'Someone' ('Someone's walking beside me / who bears my name / an amused look on her face'). Her shorter poems hit us with singularly powerful images, as in 'Snail Shell': 'I'm coiling like / an old tree / around time'.

This wrangling of dispossession, aftermath and resistance continues into the fourth and final part, which dwells on family and the poet's innate connection to Palestine, as in 'Our Bags Are Always Ready': 'From very ancient memory / I know this land / this warmth / this moisture / I felt them in my mother's womb'.

Sandwiching Elias's words are a glowing introduction by Najwan Darwish and a thoughtful translator's note by Kareem James Abu-Zeid. Darwish, a leading contemporary Palestinian poet, brought Elias to the attention of his long-time translator, Abu-Zeid, who has sensitively translated Elias in this first English collection. It is difficult, then, not to view Elias's poetics in conversation with Darwish's – and indeed both employ an incisive language that draws on physical memory, wide reading and a depth of compassion. Fitting, then, that Darwish's translator should now become Elias's. Through the shared medium of Abu-Zeid's translations, the poetics of two contemporary Palestinian poets are brought into a direct conversation, which might otherwise have been lost between the Arabic and the French.

I am unsure, however, whether the book has benefited from the parallel translation text. While parallel texts are always welcome for students of translation, they prevent the translation from standing on its own terms: we cannot help comparing the two, and the aesthetic of a mirrored image is overwhelmingly appealing to our pattern-seeking brains, so that we are quicker to judge the artistic and necessary license of the translator than

if the English text stood alone. Having said that, Abu-Zeid's translation is an excellent rendering of the poet in English, and while elements of his translation style are present, the poems remain unquestionably Elias's.

The poems' words elegantly shift from high metaphor to journalistic reflection. The reader immediately notices Elias's approach to punctuation, which is almost entirely absent in favour of disruptive line breaks. It is this absence that punctuates her poems, at times leaving the reader uncertain where a thought begins or ends, encouraging us to sit with the words, and find sense and address our own dislocation.

This collection stands out for its seething but understated anger. Elias's every word, literary reference and contextual cue exposes and addresses the wounds of occupation and exile. This is a patient book which poses its mysteries to the reader at a controlled pace, as with its two contradictorily-titled poems, 'Traveller with No Bags' and 'Our Bags are Always Ready', one near the beginning and the other near the end.

In the ars poetica of 'Every Night, Morning', Elias expresses the totality of her resistance and rage, distilled and gendered female: 'every morning it [the poem] washes / a patch of blue sky / in this extreme laboratory / of high-tech / terror'. In 'Extension of Territory' she styles herself 'OE, citizen-scribe of occupied Palestine and of the world'. The title fits her perfectly.

A Shape to Be Broken

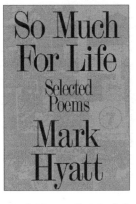

Mark Hyatt, *So Much for Life: Selected Poems*, edited by Sam Ladkin and Luke Roberts (Nightboat Books) $19.95
Reviewed by Ian Seed

I first came across Mark Hyatt's poetry in *Poetry Review* in 1975 in my school library. Peter Riley supplied this note: 'Mark Hyatt was born in 1940. His poems were just beginning to appear in magazines and anthologies when he died in 1972. He left behind a large amount of unpublished work, from which the poems in this issue are taken; there are plans for a collection of his work, hopefully to be published in 1975.' The five poems in *Poetry Review* took me tantalisingly into Hyatt's world, a world which as a lonely, frustrated adolescent I identified with. There was a sense of boredom and waiting, with an underlying tone of both menace and quiet hope, conveyed in simple, self-deprecatory lyrics:

it's very hot
butterflies knitting
on tall green plants
the common fly
buzzing in black dashes
in the orange tree
hardly moving
distant sounds murmur [...]

there's a small spider
walking over
over
('Small Things')

A Different Mercy, a chapbook of Hyatt's poems edited
by Nigel Wheale and David Trotter, was published in an
edition of 250 copies in 1976, but there has been little
since then. It seems like some kind of miracle, therefore,
that Nightboat Books, almost half a century on, have
published a two-hundred page collection, along with
Sam Ladkin and Luke Roberts's illuminating introduc-
tion, comprehensive bibliography and painstakingly
detailed set of editorial notes.

The introduction sets Mark Hyatt's poetry within the
context of his life. Hyatt was born in 1940 in Tooting. His
father, James Hyatt, worked in in a scrapyard and as a
street-seller. His mother, Rachel Hilden, was Romani,
and died when Hyatt was five. 'I'm half gypsy and I burn
with colour / like a fat cow dancing in the sun' ('Half
Breed'). His father remarried soon after. He grew up illit-
erate, working alongside his father in the market from
an early age. He was frequently beaten: 'Even as a man
I still move under the shadow / of a woman's belt or a
father's wooden plank' ('True Homosexual Love'). It was
in a gay club in Soho in 1960 that Hyatt met the writer
Cressida Lindsay. Soon afterwards, he moved with her
to Notting Hill, and through her met a bohemian set of
artists, actors and writers. Hyatt and Lindsay had a child
together. Their relationship lasted until the mid-1960s,
and Lindsay taught Hyatt to read and write.

Reading and writing quickly became the most import-
ant endeavour of Hyatt's life. As well as hundreds of
poems and drafts of poems, he wrote a novel, *Love, Leda*
(published earlier this year by Peninsula Press), which
paints a fascinating portrait of a lost world of queer,
working-class life in Soho before the Sexual Offences Act
of 1967. Hyatt died by suicide in April 1972, taking an
overdose of pills in a cave in rural Lancashire. As men-
tioned above, little of his work was published during his
lifetime, though he had his supporters, including
Michael Horowitz, Dave Cunliffe and J.H. Prynne. With-
out the interest of the latter, who xeroxed an extensive
number of Hyatt's poems for safekeeping in Cambridge
shortly before Hyatt died, most of the work would have
been lost.

Like the novel, Hyatt's poems navigate his search for
love, liberation and sexual fulfilment, and at the same
time his attempt to come to terms with the past of his
childhood and teens, as well as to overcome his perma-
nent sense of loneliness. Love and sex are pursued as a
kind of cure:

I tried to look for a body
to take home to bed
for the warmth of another body
and to have more legs under the sheets
to feel love pressed upon me
and to let the axe of time jump out of me
or to let dirt and desire do their best
to restore my mind
('I tried to look for a body')

On occasion, Hyatt's directness can weaken the effect
of the poetry. To use a creative writing tutor's cliché,
there is too much 'telling', not enough 'showing'. At
these times Hyatt does not so much take us into his
world as encourage us to feel sorry for him. As Hyatt
himself observes, 'It's hard to sell loneliness' ('Poor
Soul'). Yet however deep the despair in this collection,
Mark Hyatt finds ways to affirm, celebrate and wonder,
for example when meditating on the simple act of read-
ing and writing:

He wonders at bright words:
are words like men

a shape to be broken
with a coughing sound?

He reads life into patterns
a bursting joy in his blood.

He sees letters clear through,
print is his feed [...]

He steals a small poem
and scars it madly.
('Delicate')

Some Contributors

Kate Simpson is an editor, poetry critic and researcher. She has edited collections for Faber, New Writing North and Valley Press and is currently a contributing editor for *Ambit*. Her anthology *Out of Time: Poetry from the Climate Emergency* (2021) was a *Guardian* Book of the Year and a Poetry Book Society Special Commendation.

Ian Seed's latest publications are *The Dice Cup* (Wakefield Press, 2022), from the French of Max Jacob, *The River Which Sleep Has Told Me* (Fortnightly Review Odd Volumes, 2022), from the Italian of Ivano Fermini, and *The Underground Cabaret* (Shearsman, 2020). *Night Window* is forthcoming from Shearsman in early 2024.

Sam Adams edited *Poetry Wales* in the early 1970s and has been a contributor to *PN Review* since 1982.

Rory Waterman is the author of three collections from Carcanet: the PBS Recommendation *Tonight the Summer's Over* (2013), shortlisted for the Seamus Heaney Award; *Sarajevo Roses* (2017), shortlisted for the Ledbury Forte Prize; and *Sweet Nothings* (2020).

Anthony Vahni Capildeo is a Trinidadian Scottish writer of poetry and non-fiction. Their work includes *Like a Tree, Walking* (Carcanet, 2021). They are Writer in Residence at the University of York.

M. C. Caseley lives in Norfolk and writes essays and book reviews for a number of publications. Recent pieces have discussed Charles Simic, John F. Deane's poetry and Louis MacNeice.

Catherine-Esther Cowie was born and raised on the island of St Lucia and now lives in the US. Her work has appeared in *TriQuarterly, Prairie Schooner* with work forthcoming in *RHINO Poetry*.

Andrew Hadfield is a Professor of English at the University of Sussex and a Fellow of the British Academy. *Thomas Nashe and Late Elizabethan Writing* is published by Reaktion.

Editors
Michael Schmidt
John McAuliffe

Editorial Manager
Andrew Latimer

Contributing Editors
Anthony Vahni Capildeo
Sasha Dugdale
Will Harris

Copyeditor
Maren Meinhardt

Designed by
Andrew Latimer

Editorial address
The Editors at the address on the right. Manuscripts cannot be returned unless accompanied by a stamped addressed envelope or international reply coupon.

Trade distributors
Combined Book Services Ltd

Represented by
Compass IPS Ltd

Copyright
© 2023 Poetry Nation Review
All rights reserved
ISBN 978-1-80-01737-2-9
ISBN 0144-7076

Subscriptions—6 issues
INDIVIDUAL–print and digital: £45; abroad £65
INSTITUTIONS–print only: £76; abroad £90
INSTITUTIONS–digital only: from Exact Editions (https://shop.exacteditions.com/gb/pn-review) to: PN Review, Alliance House, 30 Cross Street, Manchester, M2 7AQ, UK.

Supported by